LOUGH SWILLY

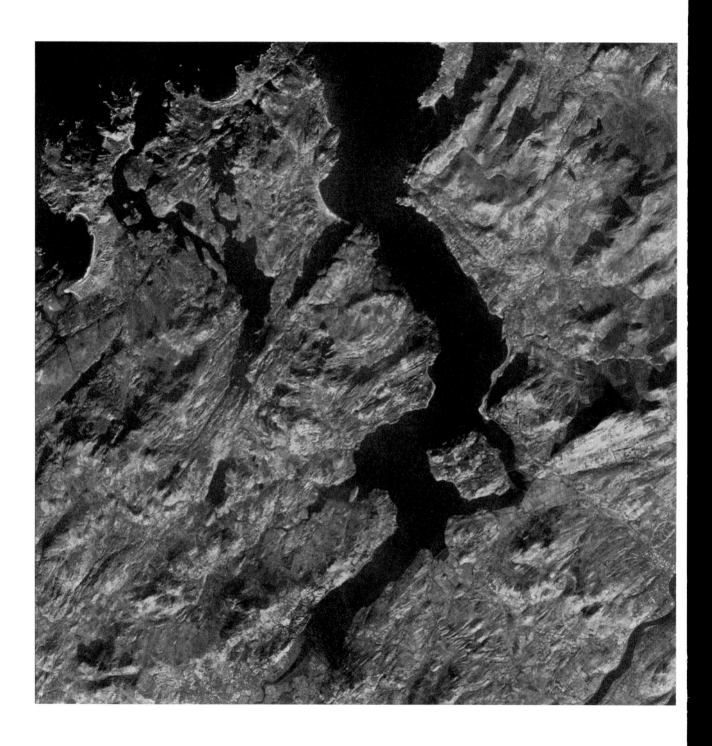

Lough Swilly from space. A satellite image reveals the Swilly's origin as a geological fault formed several hundred million years ago, exploited by ice during the past two million years and with deposits from that era preserved as a thin veneer on the lowlands. The modern lough was formed as sea level flooded the glacial valley during the past 12,000 years. The human imprint on the landscape is younger than 9000 years.

LOUGH SWILLY

A Living Landscape

Andrew Cooper

EDITOR

FOUR COURTS PRESS

Typeset in 11.5 pt on 14 pt Fournier by
Carrigboy Typesetting Services for
FOUR COURTS PRESS LTD
7 Malpas Street, Dublin 8, Ireland
e-mail: info@fourcourtspress.ie
and in North America for
FOUR COURTS PRESS
c/o ISBS, 920 NE 58th Avenue, Suite 300, Portland, OR 97213.

A catalogue record for this title is available
from the British Library.

ISBN 978–1–84682–307–7

Printed in Spain
by Grafo, S.A.

Contents

Abbreviations

BOD	Biochemical Oxygen Demand
CBAIT	Cross-Border Aquaculture Initiative
CLAMS	Coordinated Local Area Management Scheme
CSO	Central Statistics Office
DAFF	Department for Agriculture, Fisheries and Food
DED	Divisional Electoral District
ED	Electoral Division
EQS	Environmental Quality Standards
EPA	Environment Protection Agency
IWDG	Irish Whale and Dolphin Group
LAT	Lowest Astronomical Tide
LGM	Last Glacial Maximum
LSAS	Lough Swilly Archaeological Survey
NPWS	National Parks and Wildlife Service
OPW	Office of Public Works
OSPAR	Oslo and Paris Convention
OSWWTP	On-site Waste Water Treatment Plant
POWCAR	Place of Work Census of Anonymised Records
PRP	Pollution Reduction Programme
REPS	Rural Environment Protection Scheme
RSL	Relative Sea Level
SAC	Special Area of Conservation
SAPS	Small Area Population Statistics
SEPA	Scottish Environmental Protection Agency
SPA	Special Protection Area
WFD	Water Framework Directive
WWTP	Waste Water Treatment Plant

Illustrations

Notes on Contributors

NEIL BASS works as a freshwater and marine biologist and environmental consultant, mainly serving the aquaculture industry, both in Ireland and further afield. He has over forty years academic and professional experience in aquaculture, from tropical shrimp culture to farming a number of finfish species, in both land-based and marine systems.

ANDREW COOPER is Professor of Coastal Studies at the University of Ulster. He has been working worldwide in the area of coastal geomorphology and coastal management for twenty-five years and has led several coastal research projects in County Donegal. He is director of the University's MSc course in coastal zone management.

PAUL DUNLOP is a glacial geomorphologist who lectures in the School of Environmental Sciences, University of Ulster, Coleraine. He has conducted research on various aspects of glacial landforms and fomer ice sheet behaviour and has published books and journal articles on both the terrestrial and marine sectors of the last British Irish Ice Sheet.

JOANNE GAFFNEY is Quality and Environmental Officer with the cross border aquaculture initiative (CBAIT), a joint venture between Northern Ireland and the Republic of Ireland.

JESSICA HODGSON has a masters degree in applied environmental science. As project manager with Donegal County Council and University College Cork she works in partnership with academic institutions and state agencies on coastal, marine and tourism initiatives for County Donegal. She grew up on the banks of Lough Swilly.

DEREK JACKSON is Professor of Coastal Geomorphology at the University of Ulster. His research interests lie in coastal processes of the nearshore, beaches and dunes. He established the University's degree course in marine science.

EMMETT JOHNSTON is the National Parks and Wildlife Service Conservation Officer for Inishowen. He has both practical maritime experience and ecological academic qualifications. Emmett is editor of the Donegal-based environmental website www.nature.ie and co-founder of the Irish basking shark survey research project.

THOMAS McERLEAN is a maritime archaeologist in the Centre for Maritime Archaeology in the University of Ulster and is a specialist in maritime cultural landscapes. He was principal author of two award-winning books on the subject, *Strangford Lough*, in 2002, and *Harnessing the Tides*, in 2007.

ROSITA McFADDEN is a research officer with Donegal County Council. She holds a bachelors degree in geography and a masters in geographic information systems. Rosita has led out on a range of GIS mapping projects on behalf of the Research and Policy Unit of Donegal County Council and Donegal County Development Board.

LORETTA McNICHOLAS is Manager of the Research and Policy Unit in Donegal County Council. Over the last seven years, she has led a number of inter-agency and cross border research projects on behalf of Donegal County Council and Donegal County Development Board. She has a bachelors degree in public administration, a H.Dip. in applied economics and a masters degree in economics.

ROWENA MOORE is a research associate at the University of Ulster. She holds a BSc from the University of Wales, Bangor, and received her PhD from the University of Liverpool. Her research area is in coastal physics and geomorphology, and she specializes in the numerical modelling of estuaries.

JOHN NIVEN is the Chief Engineer of HMC *Vigilant*, one of the UK Border Agency's vessels that carry out anti-drugs patrols in UK coastal waters. From 1970 to 1998 he fished in Lough Swilly, mainly for salmon and lobsters, and also ran sea angling trips and the annual August Monday ferry from Inch Island to Rathmullan regatta.

MARIANNE O'CONNOR is a research assistant on the IMCORE project at the University of Ulster. She is from Donegal and has studied marine resource management at Herriot Watt University, and the University of Ulster. Her PhD from the University of Ulster focussed on the processes and management of Donegal beaches.

ANDREW SPEER works as a conservation ranger for the National Parks and Wildlife Service in Donegal. He is directly involved with 'on the ground' protection of its natural heritage. He and his family are passionate about the coastline of Ireland and spend most of their spare time exploring and enjoying it.

Acknowledgments

This work was undertaken under the Interreg Northwest Europe project IMCORE (Innovative Management for Europe's Changing Coastal Resource). This project has received European Regional Development Funding through INTERREG IVB. The IMCORE partners in Ireland, UK, France, Belgium and the Netherlands have been working together to assess the impacts of climate change on the coast and consider what steps are necessary to adapt to these changes. Staff of Donegal County Council and the Centre for Coastal and Marine Research at the University of Ulster focused on Lough Swilly as a case study.

Jessica Hodgson acknowledges the following for their help: Lough Swilly Yacht Club, Inishowen Sub Aqua Club, Inland Fisheries Board, RNLI, Rathmullan Enterprise Group, Just Kayak, Údarás na Gaeltachta, Irish Whale and Dolphin Group, and colleagues in Donegal County Council. Rosita McFadden and Loretta McNicholas thank Mícheál Ó hEanaígh, Director of Community, Culture and Planning, Donegal County Council, for his guidance in preparing Chapter 6. Neill Bass thanks Marine Harvest Ireland for the use of their data and other proprietary information. He also acknowledges the help received over a number of years from Adrian Bell and Naomi Shannon of RPS in Belfast in achieving a fuller understanding of the impacts of aquaculture on Irish coastal waters. Thanks are extended to all contributors of photographs, in particular Nigel McDowell, whose photographs help bring the Swilly to life on these pages. We thank Kilian McDaid for drafting several of the diagrams.

Foreword

Surrounded by the scenic hills of north Donegal, Lough Swilly is one of the jewels in the crown of Ireland's landscape. That landscape has been shaped by geological forces over millions of years and the lough bears the clear imprint of the last great ice sheet that covered Ireland until only a few thousand years ago. Since the ice left us, the lough has become home to a rich diversity of plants and animals, many of which use it as a stop-off point on migrations that cover half the globe. The lough provides a calm harbour from the ravages of the North Atlantic and has been an important stopping point in the North Atlantic maritime trade routes. It has been the site of important events in the country's history, in particular the Flight of the Earls.

Lough Swilly has attracted people to its shores for centuries to live, work or simply visit. From Stone Age monuments, through Medieval churches, Napoleonic fortifications to Victorian seaside resorts, human activities have left their mark on the landscape. The landscape continues to change as human activities come and go and it is rightly called a 'living landscape'; for example, some of the agricultural land that was so carefully drained and cultivated in the nineteenth century is now of such little value that it is being reclaimed by the sea. In contrast, in other parts of the lough we continue to build sea defences to protect houses and roads.

This wonderfully illustrated book gives the reader a glimpse into the rich resources of the lough and will enable both resident and visitor to appreciate the beauty and richness of this wonderful waterway. Professor Cooper and his co-authors have many years of experience and knowledge of Lough Swilly which is brought together in this book to give an overview of the lough's many values. There are, however, many challenges if the lough is to continue to be valued by society. The pressures it faces are more varied and more intense than at any time in the past, mainly because it is more accessible but also because of a bigger range of competing activities. There are also important challenges from the effects of climate change that pose difficult choices for us.

The sustainable development of the county's marine resources is a priority for Donegal County Development Board and Donegal County Council; this book reminds us of what a rich resource Lough Swilly is and encourages us to take an integrated approach to managing it for the optimum benefit of us all.

COUNCILLOR CORA HARVEY
Mayor of County Donegal

Chapter 1

Geology and Geomorphology

Rowena Moore, Andrew Cooper, Paul Dunlop and Derek Jackson

Introduction

The physical landscape of Lough Swilly is the base on which all other resources are developed. The landscape that we see today, however, has been shaped by geological processes operating over almost a thousand million years of the Earth's history. For the last two-and-a-half million years the area has been periodically covered with ice and it is less than 20,000 years since Donegal emerged from under its thick cover of ice sheets and glaciers. Against this, human activities, stretching back a mere 9,000 years, constitute a very recent imprint on the landscape.

The modern landscape continues to change under the influence of meteorological action (changing temperatures, winds etc.) and hydrological action (waves, tides, river flow etc.), which act on the underlying bedrock and loose sediments.

Solid Geology: The First Thousand Million Years

Around Lough Swilly solid bedrock is well exposed at many locations, particularly along the shore but also in the surrounding high mountainous areas. The rocks of north Donegal are mostly composed of Dalradian meta-sedimentary rocks. These very ancient rocks were originally deposited as sandstones and mudstones in shallow marine environments 600–700 million years ago but were altered (metamorphosed) during the Ordovician Period (450–500 million years ago) when large land-masses collided during a period known as the Caledonian orogeny (mountain-building period). During this period of geological upheaval the rocks were deformed and recrystallized into 'metamorphic' rocks known as schists and quartzites.[1] These rocks were further modified during the late Silurian and early Devonian Periods (390–420 million years ago) when granitic intrusions (granodiorite) rose through the Earth's crust and solidified at some depth below the surface.

These rocks have been exposed by weathering and erosion to varying degrees, and are visible at various places around Lough Swilly. In general, the more resistant rocks (granodiorite and quartzite) form high ground and coastal cliffs while the schists and pelites are more readily eroded and therefore occur in contemporary depressions. The geological map shows that the rocks have a south-west to north-east alignment, which reflects the orientation of the main geological faults.

1 Geological description of Lough Swilly is based on C.B. Long & B.J. McConnell, *Geology of North Donegal* (Dublin, 1997).

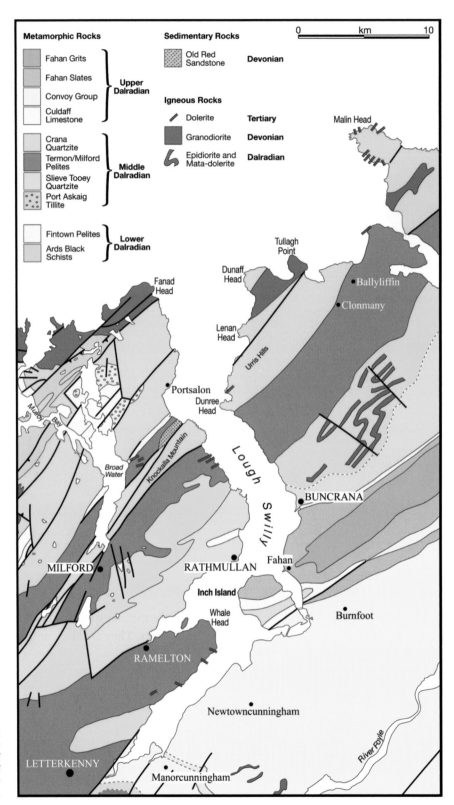

1.1 Simplified geological map of the Lough Swilly area. Based on Sheet 1 of the 1:250,000 Map of Ireland, Geological Survey of Northern Ireland (1985).

1.2 Great Pollet Arch, eroded into granodiorite outcrop on Fanad Head. Photo: Nigel McDowell.

Granodiorite is exposed in cliffs near the mouth of the lough at Fanad Head and just south of Dunaff Head on Inishowen. The Slieve Tooey Quartzite forms a band of high ground that runs south-west to north-east from just south of Fanad Head to Portsalon, and from Dunree Head to Leannan Head on Inishowen where it forms the Urris Hills. Quartzite is a hard metamorphic rock with a very high resistance to weathering and erosion. Some sedimentary features such as rippled beds and cross-stratification (which indicate original deposition in a shallow water environment) can be seen in the Slieve Tooey Quartzite.

Moving up-estuary, the next major formation is the Termon or Milford Pelites or Schists. Schists are foliated (flakey) medium-grade metamorphic rocks while pelites are their more lightly metamorphosed equivalents. They are black or grey, often with a silvery appearance due to light reflecting from mica produced during their metamorphosis. Further up-estuary is the Crana Quartzite that extends to Ramelton on Fanad and Buncrana on Inishowen. Within the Crana Quartzite are several bands of pre-Caledonian dolerite that have been folded and deformed along with the rocks into which they are originally intruded. Beyond Ramelton the Termon Schists extend to the head of the lough at Letterkenny.

At Buncrana there is a narrow band of the Culdaff Limestone, which is replaced to the south by slates (low grade metamorphosed mudstones) of the Fahan Group. Limestone is a soft sedimentary rock formed mostly of calcite. It is easily

1.3 View of the coast north of Dunree, showing the high ground of the Urris Hills composed of the resistant Slieve Tooey Quartzite. Photo: Andrew Speer.

1.4 (*opposite*) Exposure of Lower Crana Quartzite north of Buncrana. The surface has been eroded during cold periods in the Quaternary to produce a flat upper surface close to the sea level at that time. Photo: Nigel McDowell.

weathered in water and weakly acidic solutions. Slates are relatively soft, foliated metamorphic rocks, which split easily into flat sheets. The slate outcrop ends at Inch Island, where a further band of Culdaff Limestone occurs. From Inch Island to the head of the estuary the geology is dominated by alternating grits and thin limestones of the Lough Foyle Succession.

Within this geological landscape dominated by Dalradian metasediments and granodiorite, are several small outcrops of more recent rock types. A small outcrop of Old Red Sandstone (Devonian Age; 350–400 million years ago) is exposed near Portsalon and there are several Tertiary (20–30 million years ago) dolerite dykes throughout the area that were emplaced at the same time as the basalts of the Antrim plateau.

From the time of their formation, over millions of years ago, all of these rocks have been subject to erosion and modification. Some that were originally emplaced deep in the Earth's crust have been exposed at the surface by the erosion of overlying rocks while others, such as the lavas that once erupted from the dolerite dykes, have been completely eroded, leaving no trace in the immediate area.

Ice Ages: The Last Two-and-a-Half Million Years

During the last two-and-a-half million years the Earth went through a series of cold and warm cycles known as glacial and interglacial periods where the polar ice caps and mountain glaciers respectively expanded and contracted. This period of Earth's geological history is known as the Quaternary, and it involved several cycles alternating between cold and warm periods approximately every 100,000 years. Currently, we are living in an interglacial period, which began around 10,000 years ago, and is referred to by geologists as the Holocene.

Each time the global climate cooled the ice caps expanded and thick sheets of ice covered large areas of the northern hemisphere. For example, most of North America was covered by the Laurentide Ice Sheet, which was about 4km thick, and much of northern Europe was covered by a similar sized ice cap known as the Fenoscandian Ice Sheet. The area where Lough Swilly is situated was covered by a large ice mass known as the Irish Ice Sheet, estimated to have been around 1km thick.

In Ireland the last glacial period began around 110,000 years ago and ended 14,000 years ago when the last ice melted. The ice sheet reached its maximum size around 27,000-to-25,000 years ago during a period known as the Last Glacial Maximum (LGM). At the LGM the ice sheet flowed north and north-westwards out of Lough Swilly onto the continental shelf north of Malin Head. Here it joined another large ice sheet that flowed from western Scotland. Together these two ice sheets combined to form one larger ice sheet known as the British Irish Ice Sheet. At the LGM this ice sheet was so large that it crossed the sea floor and reached the edge of the continental shelf about 100km north-west of Malin Head. Recent seabed mapping has revealed a sequence of large ridges up to 35km long, 1km wide and 14m high, known as end moraines; they mark the end position of the former ice sheet on the sea bed.[2]

As well as leaving its imprint on the sea bed, there is also evidence of the work of the last ice sheet, on the landscape surrounding Lough Swilly. The hills either side of the lough have been rounded and smoothed by the ice sheet which carried rock debris at its base and was very effective in eroding the underlying rocks. Long linear scratches, known as glacial striations, have been left behind on polished bedrock outcrops in many locations. The orientation of these striations can be used to work out the direction in which the ice flowed. Another type of landform known as a drumlin can also be used to show the direction of former ice flow. Drumlins are small elongated hills, 10–50m high and generally a few hundred metres to 2km long, that are formed at the base of the ice sheet as it flows across soft sediments on the landscape. Just like striations, the longest axis of a drumlin also points in the direction that the ice once flowed. Drumlins can be found on both sides of Lough Swilly and there is a swarm of drumlins on the Fanad Peninsula that record northerly ice flow across Mulroy Bay and towards the coast. An isolated drumlin

2 See Dunlop et al. (2010) in the Further Reading section.

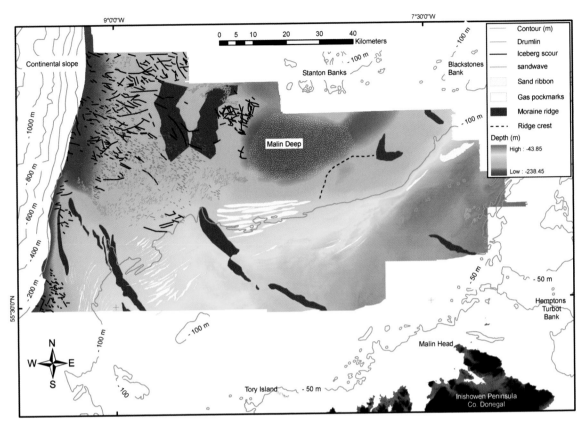

1.5 Geomorphological interpretation of the seabed between 55° 29' N and 56° 17' N, showing all the glacial and glacially related features and the major tidal current bedforms identified. The submerged moraines mark the limits of the ice sheet at various stages in the last Ice Age. (Bathymetric data from Joint Irish Bathymetric Survey.)

on the main Derry road near the fire station in Buncrana also records northerly ice flow up the main axis of the Swilly. These glacial landforms indicate that the valley in which Lough Swilly is located was scoured out by ice during each glacial period and that ice flowed northwards into the sea.

During an ice age the ice sheets are nourished by water that is evaporated from the oceans and falls onto their surface as snowfall. Over time, this snow turns to ice and becomes incorporated into the ice sheet. During ice ages vast quantities of water are taken from the oceans into the ice sheet and as a result, global sea levels fall. During the Quaternary period sea level around the globe was about 100–120m lower than it is today. During an interglacial period the climate warms sufficiently enough to melt the ice again, 'unlocking' the water, which in turn leads to rising sea levels. The sea level rise that occurred immediately after the last ice age is known as the Flandrian Transgression, and during this time many of the valleys and indentations formed by glaciers were subsequently inundated again, forming a tidal inlet known as a fjord.

As the ice retreated it left a landscape of distinctive sediments and landforms that provide clear evidence of its presence. The bed of the lough is now uniformly blanketed in the sediments left behind by the former ice sheet as it melted and retreated inland in the direction of Burt. Over 100m thickness of sediment has been deposited in the lough, and as a result, hardly any bedrock is exposed on the floor of the lough.

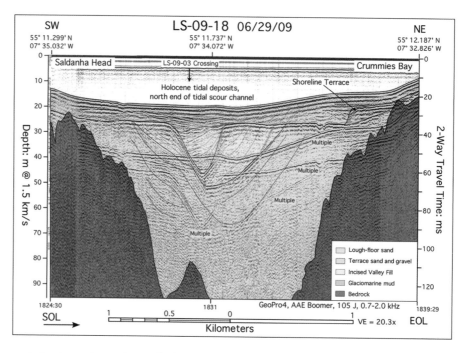

1.6. Interpreted seismic section through the lough floor (courtesy of Dr Dan Belknap, University of Maine, USA), reveals the great depth of the bedrock valley scoured by the ice and records a sequence of events including rapid sediment deposition from the retreating glacier, valley cutting by glaciers confined to the Swilly, subsequent infilling by more sediment, erosion during the Holocene rise in sea level and deposition from modern rivers.

Seismic sections through the bed of the lough reveal the topography of the underlying bedrock. Within the sediment cover are various surfaces that record various phases in the evolution of the lough during, and since, the end of the glaciation, related to the melting of the ice, changing sea levels, changing climate and influxes of sediment from the retreating ice sheet.

The geomorphology of the region clearly shows that glacial processes played a major role in shaping the lough as it can be seen today. However, the former ice sheet continues to influence the region in a number of ways. First, the great weight of the ice depressed the earth underneath it, and after the ice melted, the land has been slowly rebounding in a process known as isostatic adjustment. This land uplift is important, because when ice melts the level of the world's oceans increases, causing global sea level rise. Around the north coast of Ireland, however, there isn't a simple rise in sea level as in other areas. Instead, the global changes in sea level have interacted with the land uplift to produce a complicated *relative sea level* history. When the land rises faster than the world's ocean, relative sea level falls and when global sea levels rise faster than the local land uplift, sea level rises.

The second important effect of the ice age was the way that sediment (gravel, sand and mud) was deposited. In areas that were formerly glaciated, much of the sediment that builds modern beaches was originally deposited by glaciers and was later reworked or sorted by waves and currents. Thus in Lough Swilly the sand that built the beaches around the lough is glacial sand that has been moved by waves from the seabed to the shore and has accumulated as beaches and dunes. Pieces of the very distinctive Ailsa Craig microgranite (a bluish granite found only on Ailsa Craig in Scotland) are often found on Donegal beaches, proving that ice carried it all the way to Ireland.

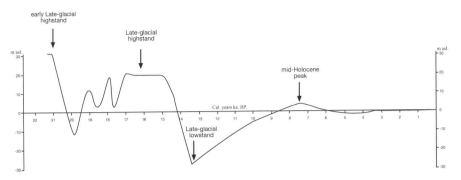

1.7 A relative sea level curve for the Swilly region. This complex curve shows the position of sea level during the past 20,000 years. Relative to the present level there have been many ups and downs of sea level that reflect local land uplift and depression associated with ice sheet advance and retreat, coupled with changes in global sea level.

Evidence of these higher sea levels during the end of the glaciation can be seen in the rock platforms around Lough Swilly. The solid rocks were eroded and planed off by waves, assisted by the cold conditions at the end of the glaciation when the sea would freeze in the winter.

The Last Ten Thousand Years

The last ten thousand years is called the Holocene. It is the time after the last ice age when the earth warmed and sea levels rose rapidly, flooding the glaciated shorelines and establishing the modern coast. In Donegal, as a result of ongoing land uplift, sea level rose higher than it is at the moment, and then fell to the present level. Historically, the tide gauge at Malin Head shows that the rate of land uplift has been about the same as the rate of global sea level rise, so that there has been very little relative sea level change in the past century or so.

The sea flooded quickly onto the land surface when the last ice melted and maximum sea level around the north of Ireland was over 20m higher than at present.[3] After this time the isostatic land uplift at as much as 6cm per year[4] caused the relative sea level to fall to about 30m lower than the present. At this time, the mouth of the Swilly might have been dry land and only a small stream flowed out to sea. The lough was flooded during the worldwide rise in sea level during the Holocene, and for a time sea level became little higher than it is at present. The most obvious effect of Holocene, sea level change is the presence of raised beaches around the lough. These beaches were deposited in the inundated areas after the post-glacial transgression and then uplifted by the ensuing isostatic response. They are best exposed at Ballyhillin at Malin Head, but there are many examples around Lough Swilly.

There are other signs of former sea levels. The peat that is exposed on the foreshore at White Strand north of Rathmullan contains the remains of trees that grew when the present inter-tidal area was high and dry. They were flooded by the rising sea level and the beach simply rolled over them.

3 McCabe (1997).   4 Kelley et al. (2006).

1.8 (*above*) Inter-tidal peat on the foreshore north of Rathmullan. The peat represents a former wooded landscape that was formed on dry land. As sea levels rose and the coastline retreated, the beach migrated across the former land surface. Photo: Andrew Cooper.

1.9 Detail of inter-tidal peat, showing tree branches and roots. Photo: Andrew Cooper.

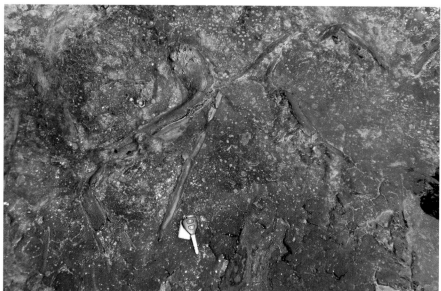

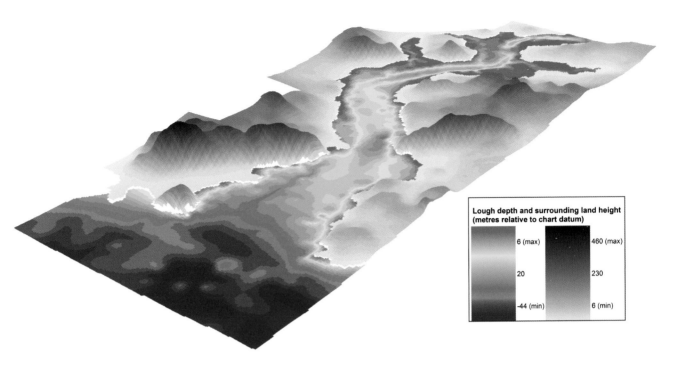

Lough depth and surrounding land height
(metres relative to chart datum)

6 (max)   460 (max)

20   230

-44 (min)   6 (min)

The Modern Lough and Coast

Lough Swilly presently covers about 150km^2 and contains around 2.05x10^{9}m^3 of water at LAT (Lowest Astronomical Tide). It is around 40km long and 7km wide at the mouth (between Fanad Head and Dunaff Head). The head of an estuary is generally regarded to be at the limit of marine influences, which in the case of the Swilly occurs roughly at Letterkenny. The lough is around 30–40m deep at the very deepest regions at the mouth of the lough, but much of it is less than 15m deep. On the basis of a seabed sediment sampling survey, the bed of the lough consists of gravelly sand at the mouth (between Dunaff Head and Fanad Head), clean sand between the mouth and just north of Buncrana, and muddy sand further upstream.

Tides and waves are extremely important processes in estuaries regarding the mixing of freshwater and marine water, the overall flushing of the system, and the movement and transport of sediment and subsequent geomorphological change. The tidal range in Lough Swilly varies between roughly 1–4m, making it a mesotidal system. The dominant wind direction is south or south-westerly or westerly. The wind-driven waves within the lough come from this direction. Ocean waves off the coast of Donegal come predominantly from the north-west, but these do not travel far into the lough. Waves generated within the lough are important in forming and maintaining the modern beaches.

Coastal zones can vary greatly in their geomorphology due to the complex interaction of the physical landscape (the nature of the bedrock, sediment type –

1.10 An oblique view of the bathymetry of Lough Swilly showing the deep region at the mouth and extensive shallows upstream.

1.11 (*above*) High sea cliffs at Leannan Head, formed by wave erosion of resistant quartzite. Photo: Nigel McDowell.

1.12 Sea caves at the base of Knockalla, formed by waves exploiting weaknesses in the bedrock. A trawler which was driven into the caves in 2009 can be seen on the right. Photo: Andrew Cooper.

1.13 A shingle and boulder beach with bedrock outcrops on the Fanad shoreline. Notice how the shingle has been carried to the top of the beach while the boulders remain lower on the shore. Photo: Nigel McDowell.

gravel, sand, mud – and sediment supply) and the dynamic processes of tidal and river currents, wind and wave action. The modern coastline of Lough Swilly reflects those differences and contains a diverse range of environments.

ROCKY COASTLINE

Rocky coasts with high cliffs in Lough Swilly are particularly well developed at Dunaff Head and Fanad Head. Some sections of the rocky coast have been eroded to form caves, stacks and arches. These, and the rock platform that extends around much of the lough, were probably formed soon after the glaciation ended when seasonal ice would have helped break down the rocks and disperse the fallen debris. Many sections of the rock coast are well-known scenic attractions such as Pollet Great Arch, Saldanha Point and the Seven Arches Caves near Portsalon.

BEACHES AND TIDAL FLATS

Lough Swilly contains a variety of beaches of different types. On the open coast either side of the entrance of the lough are some sand and gravel beaches. On Fanad they include Ballyhiernan and a number of small beaches around Fanad Head. On Inishowen there are well-developed beaches at Dunaff, Tullagh Strand, Pollan Strand and Five Finger Strand.

1.14 A beautiful view of the beach at Portsalon from the road over Knockalla. Photo: Nigel McDowell.

Between the entrance to the lough and Inch Island are many sandy beaches. They are generally located in small embayments surrounded by bedrock. The beaches on the Inishowen side include Leannan, Crummies Bay, Stragill Strand, and then a series of beaches that run from Buncrana to Lisfannon and the mouth of Fahan Creek. Mill Bay is a small beach on Inch Island. Beaches on Fanad include Doaghbeg, Drumnacraig, Portsalon/Ballymastocker, Glen Bay, Griffins Bay, White Strand (Lehardan) and Kinnegar (Rathmullan). Portsalon Beach once achieved the distinction of second place in an *Observer* newspaper survey of the world's most beautiful beaches.

Many of the beaches have interesting stories to tell. There have been dramatic shoreline changes between Buncrana and Lisfannon, for instance. There, beaches and dunes have been eroding in the north (resulting in the golf course having been protected with rock armour), but growing in the south as sand is carried along by waves in longshore drift. Ironically, a marina has been constructed at Fahan where the sand accumulates. A railway embankment that was once under wave attack, and a former diving platform on the rocks at Fahan, are now separated from the sea by more than 100m of sand dunes and beach that have formed in the past century. These changes are driven by longshore drift towards Fahan, but they may have been assisted by the blocking of Fahan Creek with reclamation walls in the nineteenth century. By slowing the tidal flows in the creek, this may have helped cause the accumulation of sand at Lisfannon.

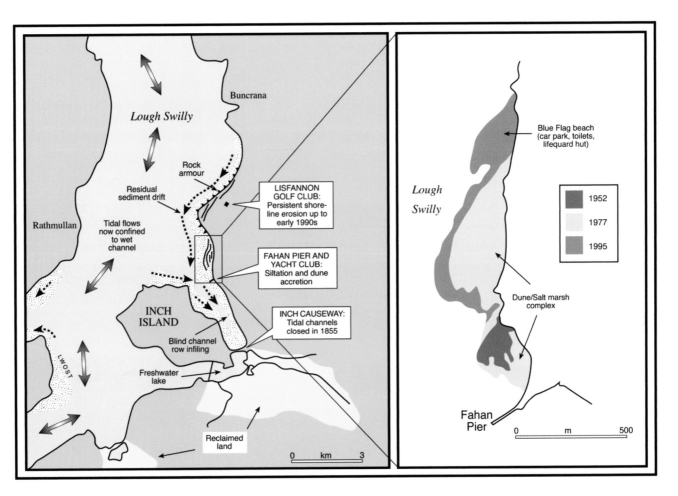

1.15 Diagram showing the shoreline changes between Buncrana and Fahan. The sand has accumulated particularly since 1950, to form the beach and dunes at Lisfannon.

The 3km-long beach at Portsalon is one of the largest on Fanad. A small river flows out to sea across the most northerly section of the beach. Over time this creek meanders south across the beach and cuts through a section of sand dunes. Eventually it flows so far along the beach that river flow cannot keep it open and then it breaks through the bar and resumes its position in the north once again. It is a perfectly natural cycle that enables the beach and stream to adjust to storms and floods.

SALT MARSH AND MUDFLATS

In the quieter waters of the upper lough and on some of the inflowing rivers are small areas of mudflats and salt marsh. These take the place of beaches in areas of low wave energy, which enables mud to be deposited and for plants to colonize the higher areas. Salt marsh is now very limited in Ireland because in pre-industrial times it was often seen as land that could be 'reclaimed' and turned over to agriculture. For this reason much of Ireland's salt marsh was enclosed behind earth walls and drained. Lough Swilly was no exception and large areas were reclaimed around Inch Island and further upstream. Small areas of remnant salt marsh can be

1.16 View along Fahan Creek toward the beach at Lisfannon. Construction of the embankment that encloses Inch Lake (in the foreground) reduced tidal currents and may have prompted accumulation of the new beach and dunes at Lisfannon. Photo: Nigel McDowell.

found at Ramelton, Lisfannon and Portsalon. The uppermost reaches of the lough have also been embanked around Letterkenny to provide flood protection to low-lying areas of the town built on the floodplain. An interesting sign of the times is that some formerly reclaimed land north of Ramelton is now reverting back to salt marsh. The sea has breached the sea walls and flooded this area of farmland. The fact that the breach has not been repaired is probably indicative of the low agricultural value placed on the land at the present time. Tidal creeks can be seen in the early stages of formation on this marsh.

Human Influences on Geomorphology

Humans can strongly alter coastal geomorphology. Man-made constructions such as sea walls, embankments, harbours and marinas all, to some extent, resist natural coastal change and when this happens the coastline responds in various ways. In the upper Lough Swilly significant land reclamation has reduced the area of salt marsh and tidal flats. Closure of the tidal channels around Inch Island has reduced the volume of water entering and leaving the inlet during one tidal cycle, and weakened the tidal currents in Fahan Creek. This might contribute to the accumulation of sediment in the creek noted in recent decades. The construction of sea walls to protect the golf course at Lisfannon has cut off the supply of sand

1.17 (*above*) Mudflats land tidal channels, like these near Big Isle, are characteristic of the upper reaches of the estuary where wave action is reduced, enabling mud to be deposited. The earth banks and drainage ditches around the reclaimed land on Big Isle are also clearly visible. Photo: Nigel McDowell.

1.18 Salt marsh is a rare habitat in Ireland since much of it was reclaimed and turned over to agriculture. This marsh at Portsalon is protected from wave action by the beach and dunes. Photo: Andrew Cooper.

to beaches at Fahan and has shifted the erosion problem to the recreational beach there. The beach in front of the sea wall has narrowed and barely any beach is now present at high tide. At the downdrift end of the same beach, reclamation and dredging associated with the construction of Fahan marina has further altered the circulation and diverted the tidal creek that drains the wetland. The past changes in the lough's form that have arisen through human activity are discussed further in Chapter 5 and the implications of future changes are assessed in Chapter 11.

Chapter 2

Coastal and Seabed Environments: Living Habitats

Emmett Johnston

Introduction

The waters and coastline of Lough Swilly are host to a wide variety of living habitats and specialist niches in which many of Ireland's rare and charismatic marine species eke out a living. These species occur in a rich variety of settings and each seeks out the appropriate balance of shelter and food resources to match their particular needs and abilities. The lough with its varied coastline and seabed contains a large number of officially described habitats, many of which are recognized as being of international importance for the conservation of particular species and/or groupings of species. They are discussed further in Chapter 7. This chapter describes the marine habitats of Lough Swilly and the diverse assemblages of plants and animals that inhabit its waters and shoreline. The lough is divided into three parts: the inner, middle and outer lough. Each part is dominated by a distinctive combination of landscape and hydrological features.

The inner lough lies between Letterkenny and Inch Island and is characterized by sheltered mud flats, known locally as 'glar', with dispersed patches of salt marsh on the western shore. Clay soils and shingles dominate the foreshore. The surrounding environs famously include much of Donegal's richest pasture, the majority of which is reclaimed or 'polder' land. Due to the input of water from the Swilly and Lenan rivers the shallow tidal waters contain a high freshwater content and many notable bivalve species including native mussel (*Mytilus edulis*) and oysters (*Ostrea edulis*) thrive in this sheltered environment.

The middle lough lies between Inch Island and Dunree Head and is characterized by a low rocky coastline indented with sand and cobble beaches. Steep heather-covered hills overlook the well-drained pastures, occasional sand dunes and woodland that outline this section of the lough. Here the lough reaches a depth of 20m in a deep-water channel running from Saltpans past Rathmullan and on through to the inner lough. Tides of over 3 knots have been recorded in this channel at springs and fishing for elasmobranch (sharks and rays) species is popular in this area. North of Saltpans and the outflow of the Crana River the lough becomes greater in width and depth and tidal currents become considerably weaker. Sand and hard clays dominate the seabed. The occasional outcrops of rock on the eastern shore provides sheltered anchorage for kelp forests and sub-tidal rock pools that host, among other species, a colourful variety of common starfish (*Asterias rubens*) and edible sea urchin (*Echinus esculentus*).

2.1 Mudflat and creek habitats of the inner lough near Big Isle. Photo: Andrew Speer.

2.2 (*opposite, above*) Rock and cobble habitats of the mid lough. Photo: Nigel McDowell.

2.3 (*opposite, below*) Sand beach habitats of the mid lough. Photo: Nigel McDowell.

The Swilly mouth or *outer lough* extends seaward from the narrows between Dunree and Saldanha Heads. The surrounding landscape is spectacularly dominated by the Urris Hills. There are inter-tidal caves and exposed cliffs over 100m high along this stretch of coast. Sandy bays indent the western shoreline and on the eastern shore there are two picturesque horseshoe beaches at Leannan and Crummies Bay. Crummies Bay is host to one of Ireland's rarest coastal habitats, established dune with crowberry (*Empetrum nigrum*) – a plant normally associated with higher altitude and exposed mountainous environs. The waters in this part of the lough are often subject to Atlantic swell from the north and the division of saline and freshwater here has a more pronounced impact on the water column than within the inner and middle catchments.

Living Habitats of the Upper/Inner Swilly

The seabed in the highly protected inner reaches of the estuary is dominated by 'glar' – a local term for the particular type and consistency of estuarine mud found on the inter-tidal flats and banks. Tidal influences are at a minimum here but the rivers Leannan and Swilly flow through the ever-shifting network of channels, tidal creeks and pans. This root-like network of channels and tidal flats forms one of the lough's most productive habitats and is home to many species of polychaete worm. These inconspicuous creatures are the foundation of the diet for the internationally important numbers of over-wintering birds that frequent these shores annually.

2.4 Cliffs and associated rocky shore habitats on Fanad. Photo: Nigel McDowell.

Bird species of note include golden plover (*Pluvialis apricaria*) and bar-tailed godwit (*Limosa lapponica*).

North of Ballybegly the main tidal channel deepens and the sediment type found on the inter-tidal zone becomes more variable. Pebbles, gravel, sand and mud all combine to create a base on which bivalve molluscs, in particular the native mussel (*Mytilus edulis*) and oyster (*Ostrea edulis*), thrive. Oyster and mussel beds in this part of the Swilly have been commercially harvested on a sustainable level for at least 400 years. Their value was deemed worthy of specific mention in the records of land entitlements during the seventeenth-century plantation and also during the first Ordnance Survey of Ireland in the early nineteenth century. Today their value is realized through the export market and a variety of traditional and modern techniques are utilized. In recent years a high-profile ecological debate has centred on the introduction of Pacific oyster (*Crassostrea gigas*) farming. The future breeding success of the native bivalve beds has become a concern with competition from independently breeding Pacific oysters cited as a possible long-term issue.

Internationally important numbers of divers and grebes use the deeper channel waters for feeding throughout the mid-tide period. At low tide deliberately scattered stones are exposed that provide an anchor for various red and brown seaweeds, and, in particular, bootlace weed (*Chorda filum*). These weeds create sheltered niches for periwinkles (*Littorina spp.*) and top shells (*Gibbula cineraria*), some of which are also harvested by hand for export. Eelgrass (*Zostera spp.*) is also present

2.5 Aerial photograph of reclaimed lands and enclosed lake at Blanket Nook. Photo: Emmett Johnston.

in the catchment area although in a dispersed and fragmented manner; migratory pale-bellied brent geese (*Branta bernicla*) and over-wintering duck often feed in this zone throughout the winter months.

The Leannan estuary west of Ramelton meanders through the Ramelton channel and contains the biggest area of salt marsh within the Swilly. The extra shelter and protection in this bay, coupled with the restriction in flow offered by Aughnish Isle, makes for constant quiet brackish water conditions. Salt-tolerant plants such as common salt marsh grass (*Puccinellia maritima*) and tufts of cord grasses (*Spartina spp.*) dominate these small areas of salt marsh, which are established on a mixed base of mud and sand. Wading birds such as redshank (*Tringa totanus*) and greenshank (*Tringa nebularia*) are commonly found feeding here.

There are three areas of reclaimed land or polder in the upper Swilly – namely, the Big Isle, Blanket Nook and the lands south-east of Inch Island (the Inch Levels). The rich mixture of alluvial soils, raised beaches and glacial boulder clay underlying this land combine to form the most productive pasture in County Donegal. The majority of these lands are now used for intensively managed winter cereals and dairy grassland, although in recent years notable crops of maize and lawn grass have been successfully grown. Complementing the winter cereal and extensive grassland is a large-scale commercial crop of potato, which provides suitable stubble feed for the early winter arrival of internationally important numbers of whooper swan (*Cygnus cygnus*) and Greenland white-fronted geese

2.6 Wet grassland enclosed by embankments at Inch Island. Photo: Emmett Johnston.

(*Anser albifrons*). In the New Year these avian giants switch to the intensive grasslands of clover (*Trifolium repens*) and perennial rye-grass (*Lolium perenne*) before making the return migration back to the Arctic. The large open field systems and managed hedgerow habitats also provide residence for many of Ireland's now-endangered farmland passerines such as the yellowhammer (*Emberiza citrinella*) and linnet (*Carduelis cannabina*). Raptors (birds of prey) such as merlin (*Falco columbarius*), sparrowhawk (*Accipiter nisus*) and buzzard (*Buteo buteo*) top the food chain in this productive habitat with notable winter utilization by the hen harrier (*Circus cyaneus*) and short-eared owl (*Asio flammeus*).

On the landward side of the embankments that enclose the polders or sloblands are artificial water catchment areas for the managed drainage of the reclaimed lands. These catchment areas form sizeable brackish lakes at Blanket Nook and on Inch Island's eastern shore between the Farland Bank, Inch Causeway and the old Tready railway embankment. The man-made water bodies have lagoon-like features because of salt-water seepage from the estuary. Extensive areas of marsh and wet grassland surround the lakes, with rushes, sedges and creeping buttercup (*Ranunculus repens*) dominating the herbaceous layer. Various wildfowl (including geese) utilize the cover and safety of the lakes and surrounding environments for feeding and, in particular, roosting. During the summer months butterflies such as the orange tip (*Anthocharis cardamines*) and green-veined white (*Pieris napi*) lay their eggs in the new growth of the flowering marsh meadows.

During drier months the runoff or drainage water flow into these two lakes is considerably reduced and areas of the wet grassland and marsh mosaic are firm enough to be grazed by cattle. Excellent conditions for breeding waders such as curlew (*Numenius arquata*) and lapwing (*Vanellus vanellus*) are created by this tightly managed practice. The seasonally lowered water table also sufficiently

2.7 Sandwich terns near Inch Island. Photo: Andrew Speer.

exposes an island of mixed sand and mud, which is topped by hardy grasses and broad-leaved herbs. It provides a near-perfect niche for an internationally significant number of breeding sandwich terns (*Sterna sandvicensis*) and black-headed gulls (*Larus ridibundus*) as well as smaller numbers of mute swans (*Cygnus olor*).

The sand and shell beach on the south-western shore of Inch Island at Mill Bay and the sand bar at Ballygreen Point reaching towards Drumboy and Blanket Nook are notable exceptions to the otherwise glar-dominated seabed. They offer a foot-hold for coarser sand-based species, more characteristic of the middle Swilly area.

Living Habitats of the Middle Lough

The middle lough is dominated by a low, rocky shore coupled with some notable long sandy beaches and this central part is overlooked by distinctive heath-covered ridges. The narrows between Rathmullan and Inch Island mark its southern boundary and Dunree and Saldanha headlands mark its northern reaches. These two narrows divide the Swilly into its three distinctive landscapes. The headland of Dunree offers extensive protection from northerly winter gales and Atlantic swell. The middle Swilly is an open water expanse, approximately 4km wide,

2.8 The junction of the Crana River with Lough Swilly. The Crana is a major source of freshwater discharge into the lough. Photo: Emmett Johnston.

dropping to depths of 10–20m. There are numerous small rocky outcrops at Colpagh, Carrickacullin and around Macamish Point.

This section has less extensive inter-tidal habitat than the inner lough and is subject to substantially more wave action and tidal influence. These factors are important in creating the distinctive habitats along its shores and within its broad marine environs, including the seabed and shoreline.

Coarse sand, gravel and mud dominate the sea floor and isolated rocky outcrops break the surface at Colpagh and Carrickacullin. They are miniature islands of permanence in this otherwise dynamic environment. The seabed offers little anchorage for surface-dwelling creatures and is subject to high levels of disturbance. Brittlestars (*Ophiura Spp.*), amphipod crustaceans (*Bathyporeia Spp.*) and polychaete worm species find their own niche here. Shallower areas host starfish species, razor shells (*Ensis spp.*), otter shell (*Lutraria lutraria*) and sea potato (*Echinocardium cordatum*). Occasional fragmented colonies of oysters (Ostrea edulis) and submerged rocky outcrops offer more productivity and often attract impressive specimens of various crab species. The highly endangered common skate (*Dipturus batis*) and spurdog (*Squalus acanthias*) famously haunt these habitats searching for the variety of bottom dwellers that are their prey. Unfortunately, discarded fishing nets along the sea floor continue to ghost fish (a term for catching fish unintentionally) and these attract a small resident population of harbour seal (*Phoca vitulina*), which stalk this area, often supplementing their diet with crabs and bivalves. Their larger cousin, the Atlantic grey seal (*Halichoerus grypus*), a once-common seasonal visitor to this section of the Swilly, is now recorded only in small numbers. As salmon stocks have reduced the seals have switched to more abundant mullet and lesser-spotted dogfish (*Scyliohinus canicula*) for their dietary needs.

2.9 The diverse inhabitants of Swilly's rock pools include pink encrusting algae, anemones, gastropods, green and brown seaweeds and many other living organisms. Photo: Emmett Johnston.

The Crana and Mill rivers provide the major freshwater influence in the middle reaches of the lough. After heavy rains the brown, mineral-enriched mountain water can be seen hugging the eastern shore of the Swilly as it drifts north, slowly dispersing and mixing as the wind and tide break its edges. The human-introduced mink has joined the native otter (*Lutra lutra*) in hunting along these river mouths and shorelines. Their diet is as varied as the territories they cover; traces of crab, fish and mussel are commonly found in the minxs' faeces. Daubenton's bat (*Myotis daubentonii*) and kingfisher (*Alcedo atthis*) also hunt the insect and fly species, which seasonally multiply along the wet banks.

Larger mammals such as the porpoise (*Phocoena phocoena*), known locally as the 'Inishowen Tumbler', can be seen from shore, following shoals of sprat and sand eel as they feed on krill and phytoplankton in the water column. Bottlenose dolphins (*Tursiops truncatus*) frequent the broad stretch of waters north of Macamish and Ned's Point. They are highly intelligent mammals who often herd balls of sprat (*Sprattus*) and sand eels along the tidal lines formed by the fronts between fresh and saline waters. These dynamic water habitats are constantly changing in salinity, temperature, turbidity and speed. Sun fish (*Mola mola*) and common dolphin (*Delphinus delphis*) are notable early autumn visitors to the Swilly.

Along the rocky shoreline low tide exposes the top of dense kelp forests and extensive areas of red seaweeds. Together these form one of the most productive habitats within the lough and any storm-cleared patches of bare rock are quickly colonized by cushion sponges, anemones and calcareous tubeworms. Topshells (*Gibbula cineraria*), starfish (*Asterias rubens*) and sea urchins (*Echinus eculentus*) graze or hunt these brightly coloured underwater forest kingdoms. Higher on the inter-tidal zone common mussel (*Mytilus edulis*) beds or bladderwrack (*Fucus vesiculosus*) and egg wrack (*Ascophyllum nodosum*) are found in large quantities. These plant and bivalve communities form shelter around colourful rock pools

2.10 The dunes, wetland and beach at Lisfannon, which have developed on the site of a former inter-tidal flat during the past century. Photo: Emmett Johnston.

overlooked by low vegetated crags. Particular parts of the shore have their own microhabitats. Colpagh Rocks, for example, is a favourite location for the harvest of edible red weeds such as carrageen (*Chondrus crispus*) and dulse (*Dilsea carnosa*), once staple parts of the Irish coastal diet. The rock pools are host to familiar creatures such as limpets, barnacles, honeycomb worm (*Sabellaria alveolata*) and the hermit crab (*Pagurus bernhardus*). On occasion small spider crabs (*Macropodia longirostris*) are trapped by the swift outgoing tide and bright sponges, dog cockle (*Glycymeris glycymeris*) or common whelk (*Buccinum undatum*) can also be found hidden amongst the mosaic of rock, sand and pool that creates a magnificent semi-submerged world of colour.

There are lengthy beaches of coarse yellow sand south of Buncrana and north of Rathmullan as well as at Stragill. The partly submerged spit or bar that extends northward in a protective arm from Inch Island is also dominated by sandy substrate although there is a distinctive mud component. These sandy areas often look barren and devoid of life but they provide excellent living conditions for a wide variety of creatures, who use the changing water depths to feed and rest in harmony with their surrounding environs. Many types of shells can be found half-buried at low tide. The otter shell (*Lutraria lutraria*) and razor shell (*Solen marginatus*)

2.11 Worm casts on the beach at Lisfannon taken from the beach giving a 'worm's-eye view' of the world. Photo: Andrew Cooper.

are particularly prominent examples. On the surface, lugworm casts (*Arenicola marina*) hint at sizeable communities of burrowing worms and sea mice (*Aphrodite aculeata*) beneath one's feet. Flounder (*Platichthys flesus*) and sand eel species dodge the attention of aerial hunters such as sandwich tern (*Sterna sandvicensis*) and gulls. The usual scattering of decaying seaweed marking the day's high water mark hosts populations of sand hoppers (*Talitrus saltator*) and sea slaters (*Ligia oceanica*) that scavenge on the debris. They, in turn, provide a valuable food source for birds such as sanderlings (*Calidris alba*).

Two small, isolated, habitats in this middle lough area are worthy of particular mention. They demonstrate the difficulty in describing habitats on this scale. South of Fahan marina an area of 'glar' with patches of salt marsh has developed under the combined protection of Inch Spit, and the Fahan and Inch causeway. These substantially reduce the degree of exposure to marine-induced disturbance. As a result this area has more in common with the inner Swilly than its neighbouring middle catchment. The other notable habitat is present on a number of beaches on Inch Island that are made up almost entirely of broken shells. Their physical form and resident species are similar to sandy beaches or pebble beaches, common in the middle Swilly, although they are unique in their makeup and visual appearance. On pebble beaches multicoloured lichens and moulds markedly dominate the upper splash zone. The underlying pebble and boulders with their often-overhanging vegetated crags provide enough consistency of shelter to allow herbaceous plants such as sea sandwort (*Honckenya peploides*), sea campion (*Silene maritima*) and sea thrift (*Armeria maritima*) to gain a foothold.

Embryo dunes and established fixed grey dunes are found at the rear of beaches in this section of the lough. Marram (*Ammophila arenaria*) and red fescue (*Festuca rubra*) grasses are the dominant vegetation. In summer the rich bryophyte (mosses and worts) and herb flora including Hylocomium splendens and thyme (*Thymus*

2.12 Typical heath habitat on the high ground around the lough. View from Dunree towards Portsalon. Photo: Emmett Johnston.

praecox) add colour and attract insect species such as bees and butterflies. Much of the dune systems back onto pastoral lands divided by native hedgerows and are generally used for cattle grazing. The overlooking heather-dominated (*Calluna vulgaris*) hilltops with patches of bell heather (Erica cinerea) and heath (Erica tetralix) are grazed mainly by black faced sheep. Exposed rocky outcrops and inaccessible areas feature crowberry (*Empetrum nigrum*) and bilberry (*Vaccinium myrtillus*) along with mat grass (*Nardus stricta*). Buzzards (*Buteo buteo*) and sparrowhawk (*Accipiter nisus*) hunt these fields and dunes for small rodents and corvid species. Irish hare (*Lepus timidus hibernicus*) are common in these surroundings and can occasionally be seen fighting in the early morning mists of March.

2.13 Flowering orchid among heath vegetation. Photo: Emmett Johnston.

Dense fog is a common occurrence along this stretch of the lough since its sheltered nature restricts the wind's ability to disperse airborne water droplets. These same aggregations of droplets provide glistening illumination to the leaves of the rich semi-natural woodlands at Rathmullan, Carradoan, Fahan and Porthaw. Having stood for many generations the compact woodlands provide a glimpse of what much of the loughs shoreline would have looked like before the advent of human activity. Sessile oak (*Quercus petraea*) and birch (*Betula pubescens*) dominate the dryer established areas while alder (*Alnus glutinosa*) and willow (*Salix. Spp.*) provide canopy over the underlying bog patches. They host a rich variety of ground flora that are typical of Ireland's peak habitat including the common wood sorrel (*Oxalis acetosella*), bluebell (*Hyacinthoides non-scripta*) and hard fern (*Blechnum spicant*). Notable residents include grey heron (*Ardea cinerea*), long-eared owl (*Asio otus*) and red squirrel (*Sciurus vulgaris*). Colonies of Leisler's bat (*Nyctalus leisleri*) and Pipistrelle bat (*Pipistrellus pipistrellus*) are common and the brown long-eared bat (*Plecotus auritus*) is occasionally found.

Humans have adapted and changed the lough side landscape in many ways to suit their needs and facilitate urban development. Hard sea defences have been substituted for dynamic dune shorelines to protect land for golf courses and urban development. Other human-induced changes including the construction of the town piers, Fahan marina, coastal walkways and residential developments, have also impacted significantly on the natural environment. These man-made structures, however, also create their own habitats that some species can adapt to, and exploit, for a successful existence.

2.14 Aerial photograph of Rathmullan Wood. This National Nature Reserve is a state-owned area of natural woodland managed specifically for the conservation of nature. Photo: Emmett Johnston.

Living Habitats of the Swilly Mouth

North of Dunree and Saldanha Head is the lough's gateway to open Atlantic waters. This is a harsh environment exposed to northerly winds and Atlantic swell. The rocky lough shores are steep and craggy. The seabed is constantly churned and washed by heavy seas and strong tidal currents. Course gravel, sand and rock on the seabed support a robust group of animal species, which utilize the crevices and holes to find shelter and escape predators like sea urchins (*Echinus esculentus*). Accumulation on beaches of coralline algae, or maerl, show that it is present on the seabed in this area. Unlike the open sea floor where only an occasional brittlestar (*Ophiothrix fragilis*) is visible, these beds of slow-growing, calcified red seaweeds covered by a thin layer of pinkish-coloured living maerl provide a stable environment for a variety of flora and fauna to flourish. The maerl beds rely on the strong tidal flow to prevent sediment particles accumulating on, or between, the maerl.

Salinity varies throughout the water column from full seawater to freshwater-dominated pockets. Long white tidal lines form on the turn of the tide as vertical and horizontal stratification of the waters occurs in all but the roughest of weather. These lines represent dynamic habitats, or fronts, and are often induced by particular headlands such as Dunaff and Dunree. The mix of salt and fresher waters,

2.15 View of Dunaff Head at the mouth of the lough. Photo: Emmett Johnston.

often with differing temperatures, creates suitable conditions for phytoplankton (floating microscopic plants) and krill (tiny crustaceans) to multiply. Shoals of sand eel and sprat are attracted to these dense accumulations of life, which can form all year round. Ireland's smallest baleen feeder, the minke whale (*Balaenoptera acutorostrata*), and the largest fish in the Atlantic Ocean, the basking shark (*Cetorhinus maximus*), also feed on these congregations of plankton in Lough Swilly. Many other shark species such as tope (*Galeorhinus galeus*), porbeagle (*Lamna nasus*) and blue shark (*Prionace glauca*) feed not on krill but mainly on the herring (*Clupea harengus*) and mackerel shoals that, in turn, are hunting the sprat.

The overlooking cliff-nesting sea birds often partake in this visual feeding frenzy with gulls, razorbills (*Alca torda*), fulmar (*Fulmarus glacialis*), black guillemot (*Cepphus grylle*) and cormorant (*Phalacrocorax carbo*) diving the Swilly's waters in search of prey. These native breeders are daily joined by the impressive Scottish visitor, the gannet (*Morus bassanus*). With a wingspan of over 2m and a specially designed skull for dissipating the impact of hitting the water surface at over 100km/hr these white divers have only one match in the air during this time. The

2.16 A Minke whale surfacing in the mouth of the lough. Photo: Emmett Johnston.

2.17 Underwater view of a feeding basking shark off Dunaff Head. Photo: Nigel Motyer.

great skua (*Stercorarius skua*), a historic visitor and recent hillside breeder on the Swilly, normally occupies itself with pursuing sandwich terns above the middle Swilly beaches but it can be attracted to large aggregations of feeding birds in the search of easy prey. The breeding sea birds nest noisily on lightly scraped perches along rock ledges and inside constricted crevices within the roofs of the huge cave formations that dominate this section of coast. Predators such as peregrine falcon (*Falco peregrinus*) and raven (*Corvus corax*) limit the success of the fledging juvenile seabirds. This rugged and remote stretch of the coast also offers shelter for newborn grey seal pups. Seclusion is important for the wool-covered pups at this

2.18 A juvenile grey seal on a cobble beach near the Swilly mouth on the Inishowen coast. Photo: Emmett Johnston.

2.19 A newborn grey seal pup at Dunaff Head. Photo: Emmett Johnston.

stage. They are unable to enter the water for the first three weeks of their lives and are completely dependent on the regular feeding visits of their mothers. Salt-tolerant plant species such as thrift (*Armeria maritima*), bladder campion (*Silene vulgaris*) and patches of wiry grasses and heath hold any sparse pockets of soil together. A species of note is the dwarf juniper (*Juniperus communis*) that is found on these cliffs in considerable quantities.

2.20 A fulmar nesting on ledges on cliffs near the mouth of Lough Swilly. Photo: Emmett Johnston.

2.21 A view of the mouth of Lough Swilly towards Fanad Head with crowberry growing in the foreground. Photo: Emmett Johnston.

Above the cliffs, blanket bog and orchid-rich upland habitats dominate with colourful bog asphodel (*Narthecium ossifragum*), round-leaved sundew (*Drosera rotundifolia*) and devils-bit scabious (*Succisa pratensis*) among the more notable plant species. Historic records of the marsh fritillary (*Eurodryas aurinia*) butterfly exist for this area but none have been recorded in recent times. Below the cliffs, within the inter-tidal cave formations and rick outcrops, colourful species groupings similar to the rocky outcrops of the middle Swilly are found. Sandy bays

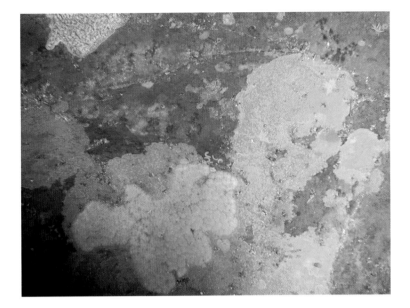

2.22 Encrusting algae on submerged rock outcrops provide surprisingly vibrant colours on the Swilly seabed. Photo: Inishowen Subaqua Club.

2.23 A crab takes refuge among the marine life on a rock outcrop in Lough Swilly. Photo: Inishowen Subaqua Club.

at Ballymastocker, Crummies Bay, Leannan and Drumnacraig break the imposing cliff shoreline. Pebble and boulder beaches also occur in indentations along the cliff base, providing a hold for salt-tolerant lichens and algae. Lightly grazed thin dune systems and blanket bog, or improved pasture, back the sandy bays. One of Ireland's rarest habitats is found at Crummies Bay; it contains fixed dune with crowberry (*Empetrum nigrum*), a plant normally associated with higher altitudes and different soil types. Juniper is again found in copious quantities here, as are extremely short swards of grasses such as red fescue (*Festuca rubra*). The rare, but acrobatic, chough (*Pyrrhocorax pyrrhocorax*) feeds in these dune slacks and along the steep coastal banks. They enjoy feeding on the leatherjackets in the cowpats and short swards, reflecting the exposed nature of the sites and dispersed grazing.

A range of submerged habitats are present on the bed of the Swilly. These include soft sediment throughout most of the lough due to the thick sedimentary infilling, but occasional submerged rock outcrops also occur along the lough margins. These were investigated at seven sites during the BIOMAR surveys of 1993. The wrecks of the numerous ships and boats that litter the Swilly sea floor also offer a limited degree of shelter and anchorage in an otherwise-exposed environment. The most notable is the *Laurentic*, which lies at the Swilly mouth. This shipwreck provides a home for fish species such as tope (*Galeorhinus galeus*) and the elusive conger eel (*Conger conger*), who hunt through the wreck's murky insides and broken portholes. The *Laurentic* lies too deep for most robust seaweeds and algae to colonize but her steel frames and spars offer a lifeline to the hardiest marine species.

Chapter 3

The Waters of Lough Swilly

Neil Bass

Lough Swilly and its Catchment

Lough Swilly is, by any measure, a substantial body of water, with a surface area of some 154km[2].[1] It is of the same order of magnitude as Ireland's other large sea loughs and bays such as Bantry and Kenmare Bays, although smaller in area than Ireland's two largest freshwater loughs, Lough Neagh (388km) and Lough Corrib (200km). Interestingly, Lough Swilly ranks high relative to Scotland's 103 defined sea lochs, running second only to Loch Fyne in terms of its length, area and water influx and fifth largest in terms of its volume.[2]

Lough Swilly meets the Atlantic Ocean between Fanad Head and Dunaff Head. It is 40km long down its main channel and reaches a width of over 5km near its mouth. Lough Swilly is actually quite shallow, with a mean depth of 11.4m at low water.[2] Its greatest low water depth is some 24m, near its mouth. At its southern end, where the River Swilly widens into the lough, it becomes shallow and inter-tidal. The mean annual tidal range of Lough Swilly is between 3.7m and 1.4m, from spring tide to neap tide.[3]

The lough is the receiving water for a total catchment area of almost 1,000km[2], excluding the area of the lough itself. A dozen or more river systems and smaller rivers discharge into the lough. All are monitored triennially by the Environmental Protection Agency (EPA) for river quality. The majority of these rivers are regarded as unpolluted but some have stretches suffering slight or moderate pollution, and even serious pollution in one case. Such impacts generally arise as the result of local agricultural run-off.

Of the largest rivers, the River Swilly discharges at the head of the lough, just north of the town of Letterkenny, while the rivers Crana and Mill enter the lough near Buncrana, on the Inishowen Peninsula, which makes up the lough's eastern shore. The largest single freshwater contributor to the lough is the River Leannan, with its lakes and tributaries. The Leannan comprises a 46km-long river system that discharges near Ramelton, on the lough's western shore. By Irish standards, the Leannan is quite a large river. Its catchment comprises one quarter of the entire catchment of Lough Swilly. It contributes almost 300 million tonnes (m[3]) of

1 Coordinated Local Area Management Scheme (CLAMS) Report (BIM, 2001).   2 A. Edwards et al., *Scottish sea lochs: a catalogue* (SMBA Special Publication 134, 1986). Unfortunately no publication defines the parameters of Ireland's loughs and bays in a similar manner.   3 C.J. Clabby et al. (2008).

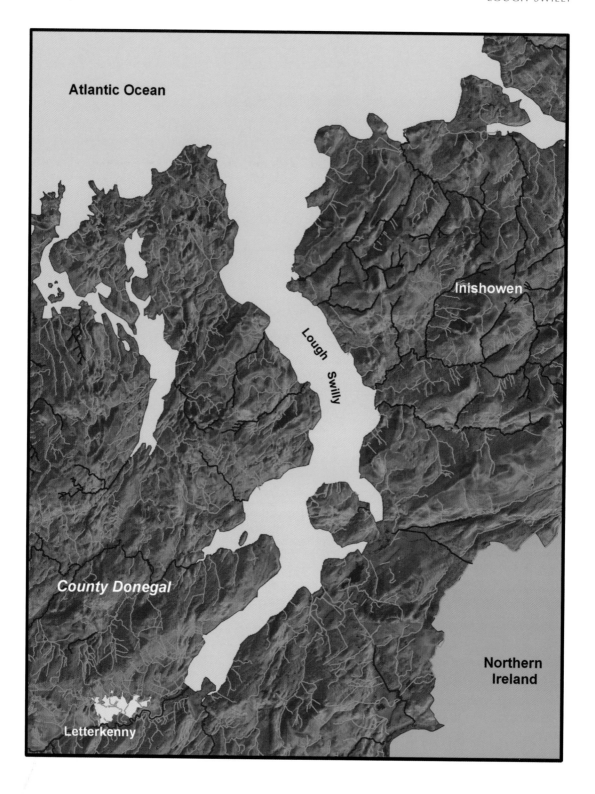

3.1 Map showing the major and minor rivers and streams that flow into Lough Swilly.

THE WATERS OF LOUGH SWILLY

freshwater to the lough every year. The River Leannan is the twenty-first-largest salmonid river in the country in terms of its fluvial habitat and twelfth largest in terms of its total lake area, its main lakes being loughs Akibbon, Gartan and Fern.

As a matter of interest, as little as twenty-five years ago, the salmon stocks of the River Leannan provided the mainstay of the commercial salmon catch of the Letterkenny District. This was easily the largest single district catch in the country at the time. The Leannan catch peaked at almost 200,000 fish in 1983. This was some 40% of the total national commercial salmon catch that year, netted from the country's seventeen Fisheries Districts. Now, like the majority of salmon fisheries, the river is closed, even to salmon angling. The country's salmon driftnets were destroyed, with the cessation of drift netting by statute at the end of the 2006 season.

About 1.45 billion tonnes (m³) of rain falls onto the Swilly catchment and onto the lough itself every year. Taking account of evaporative transpiration, from vegetation within the terrestrial portion of the catchment, this results in an estimated total freshwater contribution to the lough of over 1 billion tonnes per annum; 875 million tonnes per annum via its numerous rivers and streams and through the diffuse seepage of groundwater along its shores, and a further 146 million tonnes per annum, that falls directly into the lough itself. This combined total of over 1 billion tonnes of freshwater makes up the net seawards flow of water from the lough. Although this is a huge amount of water by any measure, it pales in comparison with the tidal movement of seawater in and out of the lough. In fact, the total annual freshwater input to the lough is little more than a single day's influx of seawater into the lough on a good spring tide!

Ebb and Flow

The tidal characteristics of the lough have been defined in a number of hydrographic surveys, the most recent of which was conducted near Anny Point in 2005.[4] Hydrographic surveys tend to be carried out over a standard fifteen days as this encompasses a full neap tide-to-spring tide cycle. Tidal height is expressed as water depth; it shows a peak tidal range, between high water and low water, of about 4.6m on the spring tide (19 September 2005) and a minimum of about 1m on the neap tide (26 September 2005). This tidal range is considerably greater than the mean range stated above, because tides at the time of the survey were approaching a seasonal maximum, around the time of the Autumnal Equinox. Such a tidal range would be considered quite large, but is nonetheless fairly typical of the west and north coasts of Ireland.

A study of the statistics of tidal flow in Lough Swilly also offers up some remarkable numbers, primarily as a result of the lough's high tidal range and its relative shallowness. Tidal influx and flushing rate can be calculated using a simple

4 Courtesy Marine Harvest Ireland.

3.2 Tidal water level fluctuation, September 2005. Tidal height is expressed as water depth; it shows a peak tidal range, between high water and low water, of about 4.6m on the spring tide (19 September 2005) and a minimum of about 1m on the neap tide (26 September 2005). This tidal range is considerably greater than the mean range stated above, because tides at the time of the survey were approaching a seasonal maximum, around the time of the Autumnal Equinox. Such a tidal range would be considered quite large, but is nonetheless fairly typical of the west and north coasts of Ireland.

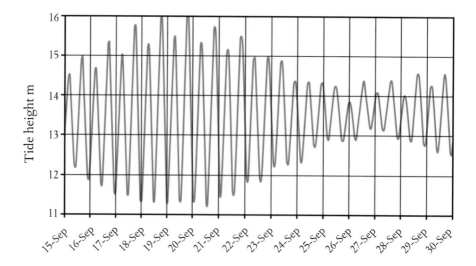

tidal prism model, calculated from the lough's area, mean depth and tidal range.[5] By this means, the total monthly tidal influx of seawater, from the Atlantic into the lough, can be estimated at about 19 billion tonnes. By way of comparison, if there are roughly 7 billion people now living on the planet and their average weight is, say, 45kg (7 stone), even the estimated daily neap tide influx into Lough Swilly, of 384 metric tonnes of seawater, is the equivalent in weight terms to the world's entire population marching into the lough every day – and as the tides go out, they would all have to march back out again!

Table 3.1: Use of a tidal prism model to calculate the mean monthly tidal influx of water into Lough Swilly.

Parameter	Notation	Data	Units
Lough Swilly area	A	154,000,000	m²
Lough Swilly mean low water depth	D	11.40	m
Thus mean low water volume	V=AxD	1,755,600,000	m³
Mean tidal range neap tide	Rn	1.40	m
Mean tidal range spring tide	Rs	3.70	m
Thus mean neap tidal volume	Pn=AxRn	215,600,000	m³
Thus mean spring tidal volume	Ps=AxRs	569,800,000	m³
Mean neap flushing time (tidal cycles)	Tn=(V+Pn)/Pn	9.14	tidal cycles
Thus mean neap flushing time (days)	Dn=Tn/2	4.57	days
Mean spring flushing time (tidal cycles)	Ts=(V+Ps)/Ps	4.08	tidal cycles
Thus mean spring flushing time (days)	DS=Ts/2	2.04	days
Mean neap daily tidal influx	Fn=V/Dn	384,037,500	m³/day
Mean spring daily tidal influx	Fs=V/Ds	860,360,265	m³/day
Thus mean monthly tidal influx	W=((Fn+Fs)/2) x30.4167	18,925,236,748	m³/month

5 Model shown courtesy Marine Harvest Ireland.

To achieve such a massive turnover of seawater, it stands to reason that currents in some parts of the lough must get very strong, particularly during spring tides. A computer model was used to investigate the water flows in the lough, based on collected, empirical hydrographic data.[6]

The model shows that flows are laminar (the water flows without turbulence) through the lough in both directions and reach maximum speeds, of around 1m/second, in the main channel of the shallow, narrow, mid-lough region, as would be expected. It can also be seen that flows are slowest in the shallowest, marginal areas and river estuaries, which also incorporate inter-tidal zones in some cases, notably at the head of the lough, in the vicinity of Letterkenny.

Currents in the main body of the lough equate to an energetic walking pace and would be considered quite fast for still-weather currents in inshore waters around Ireland and Britain.

These currents have a crucial role in the maintenance of environmental conditions in Lough Swilly and in its *carrying capacity*, that is, its capacity to assimilate environmental impacts (from its catchment; see below) without noticeable, irreversible or long-term deleterious change. To illustrate this, if we assume that individual water 'cells' and their contents are moved by the tide, in the main body of the lough, at a mean current velocity of, say, 0.5m/second, then they have the potential to travel up-lough or down-lough by over 10km on a single flood or ebb tide. The effect of this is mixing, on a grand scale, of Atlantic waters with lough waters as the tide rises, followed by the flushing out of mixed waters as the tide falls. This does not bring about an instantaneous cleansing of the entire lough but is a dynamic process that maintains conditions throughout the lough at a level driven by the huge quantities of new ocean water that enter the lough on every tide.

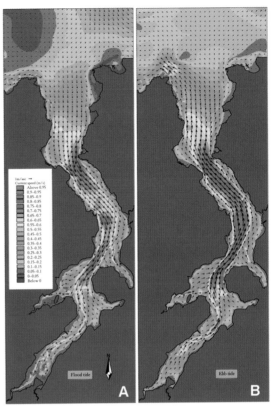

3.3 Outputs of the hydrodynamic model showing peak spring tide currents during flood tide (A) and ebb tide (B).

Winds and Wave Climate

Bearing in mind the speed of still-weather currents in some parts of the lough, it is perhaps fortunate that Lough Swilly does not face into the prevailing (most common) wind direction, as do the majority of Ireland's bays, which are along the west coast. In fact, Swilly faces broadly north and, as such, its topography largely protects it from prevailing conditions. A wind rose for the Lough Swilly area clearly demonstrates that both the commonest winds and the strongest winds blow

6 Courtesy Marine Harvest Ireland.

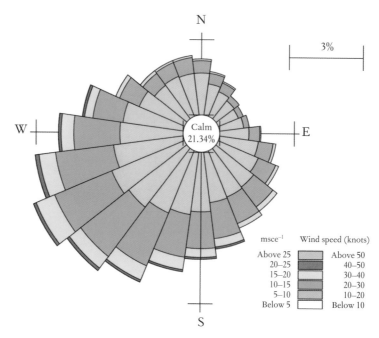

N

3%

W

E

Calm
21.34%

msce⁻¹   Wind speed (knots)

	Above 25		Above 50
	20–25		40–50
	15–20		30–40
	10–15		20–30
	5–10		10–20
	Below 5		Below 10

S

3.4 Wind rose showing the
dominant wind direction
from the southwest.

from the sector between westerly and southerly. Northerly winds, on the other hand, blow for less than 10% of the year and are quite weak, rarely reaching 30 to 40 knots.[7] Indeed, the wind rarely blows down the lough above Beaufort Force 4 (11 to 15 knots; moderate breeze) for long enough to have any major impact on tidally generated current speeds.

This relatively benign wind climate is reflected to some extent in the wave climate in the lough, although the wave climate is, in fact, dominated by storm conditions approaching the lough from the Atlantic, with only a minor contribution from waves generated by local wind conditions. A wave climate projection for a 1-in-50 year return period storm (a storm with a force that will be experienced only once every fifty years) has been undertaken. A 1-in-50 year return period storm is normally taken as a measure of possible extreme storm conditions in the modelling of wave climate predictions for an area; in any one year though there is a 2% (1-in-50) chance that such a storm will occur! The most recent storm of this magnitude to hit Ireland and Britain was probably Hurricane Charlie in 1986.

Swilly's worst storms will always approach from around north-north-west. The in-lough wave climate resulting from storms approaching from any other sector will be mild by comparison, as a result of the sheltering topography of the Fanad and Inishowen peninsulas. The worst storm conditions occur in the mouth of the lough, where shelter is the least. Here, wave height (peak to trough) is projected to exceed 7m. By comparison, the worst-case conditions off Anny Point can be expected to be no worse than quite mild, with a peak wave height of about 3.7m

7 Winds of 30 to 40 knots =15–20m/second or Beaufort Force 7–8, near gale to gale force. Prevailing winds, on the other hand, would reach Force 9 to 10, strong gale to storm force, on occasions.

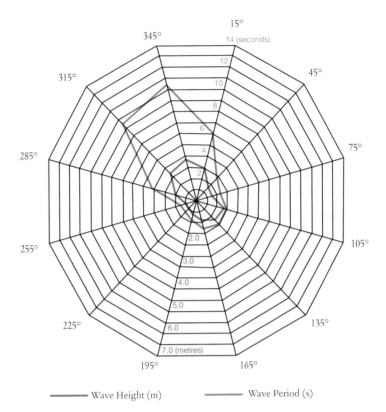

Wave Height (m)   Wave Period (s)

3.5 Significant wave height, mean wave period and storm direction for a 1:50 year storm in the vicinity of Anny Point.

3.6 Simulated significant wave height and mean wave direction for a 1:50 year worst-case storm scenario. Such conditions would occur when a 1:50 year Atlantic storm enters the lough from 345°, which is just north of NNW (North is 360° and NNW is 337.5°).

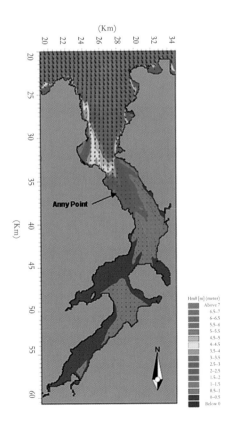

and a wave period of about 10.5 seconds. Further, even in a 1-in-50 year return period storm, the wave climate towards the head of the lough decreases to not much more than a ripple, south of the shelter provided by the twist in the lough's axis north of Rathmullan.

In fact, projections show that there is very little difference in magnitude between a 1-in-50 year return period storm and an average storm (return period 1-in-1 year), again due mainly to the lough's sheltering geography and topography. Thus, although some fishermen, sailors and fish farmers may disagree, while currents run fast in some areas, wave climate in much of Lough Swilly is, for the most part mild, with nothing more than the irritation of short wavelength, very choppy waves, most frequently caused by local, rather than Atlantic, wind conditions.

Similar predictive wave climate models have been generated for west-facing bays such as Kenmare Bay and Bantry Bay. While broadly similar to Lough Swilly, in that their mouths are as open to the Atlantic, these bays are exposed to prevailing conditions from the west to south-west, and therefore experience storms that are not only much more frequent, but also much more violent, with waves of up to twice the height of those expected for a 1-in-50 year return period storm in Lough Swilly.

Lough Swilly as a Receiving Water

No study of the waters of Lough Swilly would be complete without examining its role as the receiving-water for the inputs that arise from the gamut of human activities that occur in its catchment. Is the lough able to disperse and assimilate these inputs or, like the North American Great Lakes at their worst, is there a threat Lough Swilly might turn into an ecological dustbin? The inputs of greatest concern are *nutrients*, which, in this context, are bioactive inorganic chemicals containing either nitrogen or phosphorus, in aqueous solution. Nutrients are required for the health and growth of plant matter, be it phytoplankton and algae in freshwater and seawater or any other plant, from grasses to trees, on land.

In an aquatic system, be it marine or fresh water, plant cells respond to the presence of an adequate balance of nutrients, along with carbon dioxide and sunlight, by growing, through the process of photosynthesis. Growth of plant material is the first step in the food chain from which all animal nutrition stems; thus plant growth is termed *primary production*. Nitrogen (N), mainly available in the form of soluble inorganic nitrate salts, is the first limiting nutrient (the one that is in the shortest supply and might therefore limit growth) to primary production in marine systems, where phosphorus is plentiful. Phosphorus (P), mainly available as soluble inorganic phosphate salts, is the first limiting nutrient to primary production in freshwater systems, where it is normally quite scarce. This is an annual/seasonal cycle in that inorganic nutrients in solution are mopped up into the organic building blocks of primary production in the spring and summer months but return into solution as inorganic nutrients once again, as plant cells die and decompose over the winter months.

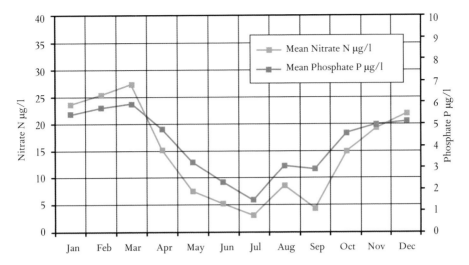

3.7 Mean seasonal nutrient data[8] abstracted from a 45-year database for the Malin Shelf Outer Area, offshore from Lough Swilly, which is monitored by the UK Fisheries Research Service.

The entire process of primary production involves a number of natural cycles – the nitrogen cycle, the phosphorus cycle, the carbon cycle and a few other, minor ones. These roll on, season after season, between the Earth's lands, waters and atmosphere.

The natural equilibrium in the aquatic environment of a receiving water can be upset if inputs from its catchment, such as nutrients, exceed its carrying capacity (that is, more nutrients are delivered than the system can assimilate). Elevated nutrient concentrations in receiving waters cause primary production to exceed its natural level – termed *eutrophication* (meaning well-fed). If the process proceeds to its extremes *hypertrophication* (over-feeding) occurs, with the long-term loss of the natural balance of organisms (and oxygen balance) on which a normal and sustainable aquatic environment depends. This was the fate of the Great Lakes region, as the result of increasing organic pollution from agricultural development, forestry and urbanization along its shores. In the context of Lough Swilly, any step down this route would be undesirable because it would cause changes in the ecology of the lough that could prove difficult to reverse.

The trophic status of the waters of Lough Swilly and its catchment was investigated in a desk study, reported to the Lough Swilly CLAMS Group in 2002[9] and updated as new data on the catchment became available. The study identified six main sources of nutrients in the lough's catchment. Each one was tracked, from its source, through the catchment, into the receiving waters of the lough and onwards to its fate in the wider aquatic environment. The six nutrient sources identified are described under the following headings:

1. NUTRIENT PRODUCTION AND INPUTS FROM AGRICULTURAL LIVESTOCK IN THE SWILLY CATCHMENT

There are two main types of livestock in the Swilly catchment: cattle and sheep. Populations of other terrestrial livestock were regarded as insignificant for the

8 Slesser & Turrell (2005).   9 Bass (2002), p. 40.

purposes of the study. Population data for both livestock and humans is collected by Divisional Electoral District (DED) in the national census. A full national census is carried out by the Central Statistics Office (CSO) every decade. The most recently available census data was published in 2002,[10] the source of the population data given in Table 3.2. The populations of cattle and sheep both exceed those for humans in the catchment. It may come as a surprise to anyone who has driven through Fanad or Inishowen that well over a quarter-of-a-million sheep graze the Swilly catchment, although numbers reduced considerably between the 1991 and 2000 censuses.[11] The census also provides livestock data by type (for example, bulls, heifers, rams, ewes), which enables a total weight of cattle and sheep in the catchment to be estimated. This is a necessary calculation step because annual nitrogen and phosphorus excretion estimates are derived from total animal weight, using factors provided in the Rural Environmental Protection Scheme (REPS) Report, published in 2000.[12] Table 3.2 gives the calculation steps for nitrogen and phosphorus production by each inhabitant group.

For all terrestrial sources, a certain proportion of the nutrients generated in the terrestrial catchment is taken up by vegetation and bacteria, before reaching the lough. Thus, except in the case of salmon, which are farmed in the lough itself, inputs of nutrients to the lough can be calculated using factors provided by OSPAR[13] documentation for Ireland.[14] Table 3.3 sets out these factors for each source and estimates the resulting inputs to the lough. Inputs from cattle and sheep are combined in this table.

2. NUTRIENT PRODUCTION AND INPUTS FROM THE HUMAN POPULATION IN THE SWILLY CATCHMENT

Total resident humans counted in the 2000 census stood at 58,744. An estimate of tourist visitors taken from Bord Fáilte data, indicated an annual mean tourist number, represented as full-time resident equivalents, of 3,708. This gives a catchment total mean annual resident human population of 62,452.

Human nitrogen and phosphorus production, including an allowance for industrial and domestic processes, was calculated much as for livestock, but using the factors provided for humans, in the OSPAR documentation for Ireland, previously referred to (see Tables 3.2 and 3.3). In the absence of any empirical data at the time that the study was last updated, the table made a general assumption that 40% of the catchment's human inhabitants are connected via a sewer main to an effluent treatment plant while 60% are rural dwellers, using septic tanks for effluent treatment.

---

10 CSO 2002. Results of 2000 census.   11 There were about 320,000 sheep in the 1991 census.   12 Department of Agriculture Food and Rural Development, 2000. Agri-environmental Specifications for REPS 2000. 13 OSPAR refers to the Oslo and Paris Convention, which is the current legal instrument guiding international cooperation on the protection of the marine environment of the Northeast Atlantic. Work under the Convention is managed by the OSPAR Commission.   14 OSPAR document NEUT 99/5/3-E 1999; written by Irish EPA personnel in 1999, based on empirical data.

New data, published in 2009, as part of Ireland's Shellfish Pollution Reduction Program[15] (Shellfish PRP) under the Shellfish Waters Directive[16] and the Quality of Shellfish Regulations, 2006,[17] broadly supports these estimates.[18] It also gives more recent and detailed information on the treatment of human waste waters in the catchment. The PRP report characterizes Waste Water Treatment Plants (WWTPs) in the nine urban centres that discharge to the Swilly catchment, namely Buncrana, Kilmacrennan, Letterkenny, Manorcunningham, Milford, Newtowncunningham, Ramelton and Rathmullan, as well as the catchment's 15,673 On-site Waste Water Treatment Plant systems (OSWWTPs), the majority of which would be known to most of us as septic tanks.

The news regarding the current state of waste water treatment in the Swilly catchment, detailed in the Lough Swilly Shellfish PRP Characterization Report,[19] makes for grim reading. The report describes the waste water treatment facilities in six of Swilly's eight urban centres as 'at risk', a term which it also applies to 98.48% of the catchment's OSWWTPs, for a variety of reasons. The report highlights waste water treatment facilities overall as the Key Pressure on Lough Swilly's Designated Shellfish Area.

A case in point is the Letterkenny WWTP, the catchment's largest plant. This has lamentably insufficient assimilative capacity, both for the present and for anticipated future loads. This is largely because Letterkenny has grown faster than almost every other town in the country over the last decade, and the expansion of its waste water treatment facilities has failed to keep pace. As a result, the Letterkenny plant is now due to be upgraded to provide secondary sewerage treatment for a future population equivalent of 40,000 people. In the meantime, however, the EPA report *Water Quality in Ireland 2004 to 2006* states:

> As in the previous reporting period, marked deoxygenating and excessive phytoplankton production was again observed in the Upper Swilly Estuary … Nutrient concentrations in the estuary and in the inflowing Swilly River were well below their respective criteria, indicating that the observed disturbance of both oxygen and chlorophyll is more than likely attributable to excessive enrichment from Letterkenny waste water treatment plant, which discharges into the upper reach of the estuary. This view is also confirmed by the elevated BOD concentrations of 8.1 mg/l (95 percentile) recorded in the estuary (… which was) the highest 95 percentile BOD statistic recorded in any of the water bodies assessed during the current period.

15 EPA 2009. Pollution Reduction Program Final Report.   16 Shellfish Waters Directive 2006/113/EC. 17 SI No. 1.3268 of 2006.   18 Table 3 estimates that 37,371 people (60% of catchment inhabitants) use septic tanks. For 15,673 septic tanks, this gives a proportion of 2.4 inhabitants/septic tank, regarded as reasonable for input calculation for this document.   19 EPA 2009. Shellfish Pollution Reduction Program. Characterization Report Number 28, Lough Swilly Shellfish Area, County Donegal.

In broad terms nutrients, chlorophyll (indicative of the level of primary production) oxygen and BOD[20] conditions at the head of the Lough Swilly, immediately down-stream of the outfall of the Letterkenny WWTP, are poor to very poor by national standards. Thankfully, however, this situation does not pertain to the open and dispersive waters of the lough as a whole, where EPA/Local Authority monitoring at two points indicates that the lough is not polluted, but characterized as 'low to very low' against the assessment level for chlorophyll and oxygen under-saturation. It is also characterized as being of 'good quality' in respect of BOD content.

A Note on Bathing Waters is justified under the heading of human inputs because bathing water quality is largely dictated by its content faecal coliform and intestinal enterococci bacteria, deriving from human and terrestrial animal excretion. These organisms are pathogenic to humans and are generally only present in any numbers as a result of inadequate treatment of human sewerage. Bathing waters are monitored for these bacteria under the new Bathing Water Regulations,[21] under which freshwater and seawater beaches with compliant waters are designated annually.

The four Lough Swilly beaches monitored in the sampling program all met the highest level of compliance, known as the EU Guide Values. Further, on the basis of a wide range of other criteria that apply, two of these beaches, Portsalon (Ballymastocker Strand) and Lisfannon, have long been classified as Blue Flag beaches. This is despite the fact that coliform levels reach critical levels imme-diately downstream of the Letterkenny WWTP, as do all other water quality parameters monitored by EPA.

3. NUTRIENT PRODUCTION AND INPUTS FROM SALMON FARMING IN LOUGH SWILLY

The most numerous inhabitant group in the Swilly catchment is farmed salmon, although the lightest in terms of individual weight. In this case, the study is based on a standing stock about 40% higher than licensed in the lough at the present time in order to project the impact on conditions in Lough Swilly should further aquaculture licences be granted. Salmon nutrient production was calculated following the methods of Davies (2000),[22] which have become the standard for the aquaculture industry; see Table 3.2. Salmon differ from all other catchment inhabitants in that they actually inhabit the lough waters. Therefore, all the nutrients that they produce pass directly into the lough, without initial partial

---

20 BOD; Biochemical Oxygen Demand; an analytical technique which determines the amount of oxygen required by aerobic organisms to decompose the organic matter in a given sample of water. The higher the BOD, the higher the level of organic pollution in the sample.   21 SI No. 79 2008, transposed from the new Bathing Water Directive 2006/7/EC, which has now superseded Bathing Water Regulations SI No. 155, 1992 as amended, transposed from the EU Bathing Waters Directive 76/160/EEC, in March 2008.   22 Davies I.M., 2000. Waste production by farmed Atlantic salmon. ICES CM 2000/O:01

Table 3.2: Lough Swilly catchment: nitrogen and phosphorus production by inhabitant type. Abstracted from CSO Census 2000 data.

	All Humans	All Cattle	All Sheep	Farmed Finfish	Total, all inhabitants
Lough Swilly catchment total numbers	62,452	77,263	285,734	1,145,720	1,571,169
Mean weight kg	55	411	50	4.5	
Max est. standing stock / biogain tonnes	3,435	31,736	14,391	2,500	52,061
Mean N produced kg per capita pa	3.2795	50.0344	7.8852	0.080	
Mean P produced kg per capita pa	0.9839	7.3016	1.2032	0.0013	
Kg N/inhabitant tonne	59.6	121.8	156.6	36.863	
Kg P/inhabitant tonne	17.9	17.8	23.9	6.186	
Total N produced, tonnes pa	204.8	3865.8	2253.1	92.158	6415.8
Total P produced, tonnes pa	61.4	564.1	343.8	15.464	984.9
N produced, tonnes pa as % of yield	3.19	60.25	35.12	1.44	100.0
P produced, tonnes pa as % of yield	6.24	57.28	34.91	1.57	100.0

assimilation in the catchment, which applies to terrestrial nutrients production. This is allowed for in the calculations shown in Tables 3.2 and 3.3.

4. AGRICULTURAL FERTILIZER USE IN THE SWILLY CATCHMENT

The use of fertilizer in the Lough Swilly catchment was estimated from statistics published by the Department for Agriculture, Fisheries and Food (DAFF).[23] This gives national fertilizer use in 2003/4 (the latest data available, when the 2002 study was updated) of 362,525 tonnes of nitrogen and 42,661 tonnes of phosphorus, or an average of 5.26 tonnes N and 0.62 tonnes P per hectare for the Irish landmass (68,890km^2; CSO). On the basis of a land use estimate of 60% for fertilized land (also excluding land used for forestry), fertilizer use in the Swilly catchment was estimated at 2,845 tonnes N and 335 tonnes P per annum. These figures are in broad agreement with estimates subsequently given in the 2009 Swilly PRP Characterization Report. Table 3.3 shows an estimate of the inputs of nitrogen and phosphorus likely to arise from fertilizer use, using the appropriate OSPAR input factors, that is, that 20% of fertilizer nitrogen and 4% of fertilizer phosphorus would enter the lough.

23 www.agriculture.gov.ie/publications/2008/compendiumofirishagriculturestatistics2008/listoftabs/

		Inorganic nitrogen inputs			Inorganic phosphorus inputs		
Catchment source	Number	OSPAR factor	Input N tonnes pa	Nitrogen %	OSPAR factor	Input P tonnes pa	P %
Humans with water treatment	24,981	0.727 x 3.287kg N pp pa	59.70		0.667 x 0.9855kg P pp pa	16.42	
Humans with septic tanks	37,471	2 x 2.5kg N pp pa	18.74		0.04 x 25kg P pp pa	0.37	
Total humans	62,452		78.43	3.73		16.80	17.62
Livestock (cattle + sheep)		0.2 x total livestock N	1,223.77	58.26	0.04 x total livestock P	36.32	38.10
Fertilizers		0.2 x total fertilizer N	580.70	27.65	0.04 x total fertilizer P	18.61	19.53
Forestry		0.542 tonnes N/km^2 pa	40.65	1.94	0.033 tonnes P/km^2 pa	2.48	2.60
Background		0.075 tonnes N/km^2 pa	84.75	4.03	0.005 tonnes P/km^2 pa	5.65	5.93
Salmon farming		Total N production	92.16	4.39	Total P production	15.46	16.22
Total inputs from catchment			2,100.46	100.00		95.32	100.00

Table 3.3: Estimated nutrient inputs from Swilly catchment to lough by source.

5. FORESTRY

A draft Lough Swilly Water Quality Management Plan was commissioned by Donegal County Council in 1999.[24] This estimated that there was 75km^2 of forestry in the Swilly catchment at that time. The Swilly PRP Characterization Report indicates that this figure probably referred to the extent of coniferous forestry only, which had increased only marginally by 2009 (0.1km^2 per annum maximum)[25] and that total forestry, including deciduous and other forest types, now stands at 117.27km^2. This figure has been used in Table 3.3 to update the calculation of forestry inputs for the catchment, using the OSPAR input factors of 0.540 tonnes N and 0.033 tonnes P per hectare of forestry per annum.

6. BACKGROUND NUTRIENT INPUTS

This comprises nutrients that enter the lough from the catchment 'naturally', in the precipitation of rainfall and dust. OSPAR uses input factors of 0.077 tonnes N and 0.005 tonnes P/km^2 for annual background nutrient inputs to receiving waters in Ireland; see Table 3.3.

Figure 3.9 summarizes the data given in Table 3.3 as nutrient inputs by percentage and also shows the total annual nutrient inputs from the catchment, as 2,100.46 tonnes N and 95.32 tonnes P respectively.

24 Coordinated Local Area Management Scheme (CLAMS) Report, BIM, 2001.   25 Pers. comm. Kevin McCarthy, Coillte, March 2010.

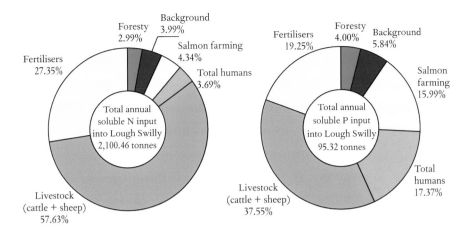

3.8 Estimated nutrient (nitrogen and phosphorus) inputs to Lough Swilly (% by source).

Lough Swilly Total Nutrient Budget

Having quantified the nutrient inputs entering the lough annually from its catchment by source, the 2002 study goes on to estimate the total nutrient budget for the lough, comprising not only catchment inputs but also the nutrients dissolved in the seawater that enters and exits the lough on every tide. The total annual nutrient budget for the lough can be estimated by multiplying the total annual tidal seawater influx of water (an astonishing 227 billion tonnes per annum; see Table 3.1) by the annual mean nutrient concentrations in the lough. These latter figures, for nitrogen and phosphorus, were derived from a historical nutrient database for monthly samples taken at a control site in the mid-lough over the fifteen-year period between 1991 and 2003 by Marine Harvest Ireland, who farm salmon in the lough. The mean concentration figures thus derived are 65.78µg/l for nitrogen and 3.86µg/l for phosphorus, which, when multiplied by the total annual seawater water influx, give the total figures for the annual nutrient budget for the lough; see Table 3.4.

It should be noted in passing that the mean nutrient concentrations given for the lough, of 65.78µg/l nitrogen and 3.86µg/l phosphorus, are higher than the annual mean levels given in the offshore nutrient datasets given in Figure 3.7. This difference is, by and large, due to the inputs received from the Swilly catchment and the nutrient equilibrium that is reached in the lough as a result of tidal flushing.

As can be seen in Table 3.4, given the total nutrient input and the catchment nutrient inputs, it is a simple matter of subtraction to derive a figure for the tidal nutrient input from the ocean and to illustrate this as a percentage of the entire budget. What becomes immediately clear is that the nutrient budget of the lough is dominated by the water and nutrients that enter the lough tidally from the Atlantic Ocean, and indeed that are flushed back out of the lough, once mixed with a proportion of the nutrient inputs from its catchment, as the tide falls. This is one sure indication that, as a whole, the lough is maintaining a healthy trophic status, by and large as a result of its rapid flushing rate. With reference to the tidal

Table 3.4: Estimated annual nutrient flux into Lough Swilly from all sources				
Source	Nitrogen tonnes	Phosphorus tonnes	Nitrogen %	Phosphorus %
Humans	78.43	16.42	0.53	0.56
Livestock	1,223.77	36.32	8.26	1.24
Fertilizer	580.70	18.61	3.92	0.64
Forestry	40.65	2.48	0.27	0.08
Background	84.75	5.65	0.57	0.19
Salmon farm	92.16	15.46	0.62	0.53
Tidal influx	12,716.79	2,826.54	85.82	96.75
Total flux	14,817.25	2,921.48	100.00	100.00

3.9 Estimated annual nutrient flux into Lough Swilly (% by source).

currents, this is, in turn, due to the shallowness of the seabed and the height of the tides that flush Lough Swilly.

Overall Condition

By way of concluding observations, just what is the state of health of Lough Swilly and its catchment and what are its long-term prospects? We can see that the nutrient sources that arise from the agriculture and forestry sector provide the greatest proportion of nutrient inputs to the lough. This is the normal state of affairs throughout the western world, wherever agriculture is commonplace. However, because agricultural inputs are diffuse and Swilly is a very hydroactive system, no significant localized impacts occur. For this reason the Swilly PRP Report does not classify agriculture as a Potential Key Pressure on the designated shellfish waters of the lough, but a Secondary Pressure.

While human domestic and industrial waste inputs to the lough are a fraction of agricultural inputs, point source impacts from WWTPs can be problematic. This is the case, for example, at Letterkenny, where a combination of WWTP under-performance and relatively poor flushing and dispersal in the immediate vicinity of the plant discharge point conspire to create significant localized impacts. This will continue to be regarded as the Key Pressure on the Designated Shellfish Area, in particular in respect of faecal coliform bacteria, until such time as the Letterkenny WWTP has been radically upgraded. Despite this, as the WWTP discharge enters the wider environs of a well-flushed lough, this problem is dissipated, to the extent that Lisfannon Beach, just 20km or so downstream of the WTTP outfall, has long held Blue Flag status.

Nonetheless, levels of coliforms, although quite low in the open waters of the lough, do represent a problem, since they are concentrated by shellfish. As a result, the designated shellfish waters of the lough are classified as Class B. This means that shellfish harvested require depuration, heat treatment or re-laying to meet Class A (minimal coliform count) standards, before they can be sold. Again, this situation can be expected to pertain until the Letterkenny WWTP is upgraded.

The Swilly PRP does not regard finfish farming as a risk to the shellfish status of the lough, despite the fact that finfish farms are point sources of inputs and discharge all their waste streams intact to the receiving waters. In the main, this is because finfish to not contain faecal coliform bacteria and because, following the steep learning curve that finfish farming has undergone in the last three decades or so, farm sites are located in very well flushed areas, relatively close to, or in, open sea conditions. In addition to this, the quality of salmon feeds, feeding efficiency and control, stock survival and growth rate, as well as treatment methodologies have all improved.

All the data reviewed in this study for nutrients, as well as, albeit briefly, for a selection of other inputs, indicate that Lough Swilly is operating within its overall carrying capacity. This seems to be confirmed by another measure of environmental quality, the use of Environmental Quality Standards or EQSs. These were initially used in the context of fish farming waters by the Scottish Environmental Protection Agency (SEPA) but now have a wider application, under which each must be reviewed over a minimum fifteen-year period before official acceptance. The established EQS for nitrogen in seawater, as originally proposed by SEPA, is 168µgN/ml. That used for phosphorus is the OSPAR standard of 119µg/ml. It can be concluded that there is no evidence that nutrient levels in the lough have ever approached these levels at any time of year.

On this basis, it appears that, overall, from the perspective of nutrients, Lough Swilly is operating within its carrying capacity but there are no grounds for complacency. There are clearly a number of issues that need urgent attention, in particular at the head of the lough. It is also clear that only an integrated approach to the future use and development, within strict environmental guidelines, will guarantee that the waters of Lough Swilly will continue to be a source of sustainable exploitation, enjoyment and livelihood for its stakeholders, as well as a place of great power and beauty, for generations to come.

Chapter 4

The Archaeology and History of Lough Swilly

Thomas McErlean

Introduction

In terms of heritage Lough Swilly is one of the great maritime cultural regions in Ireland, and as the scene for some of the great maritime events in the island's history, it can rightly be regarded as one of Ireland's major historic seascapes. Among these sea-related events is the iconic episode known as 'the Flight of the Earls' in 1607, when some of the leading Gaelic aristocracy boarded a small vessel at Rathmullan and sailed out of the lough into exile. This marked the end of the Gaelic way of life and set the scene for the Ulster Plantation. In the 1790s the lough was at the forefront of the great national fear of an invasion from Revolutionary France and was heavily fortified. By 1812 the threat of a Napoleonic invasion intensified and state-of-the-art defensive installations were put in place around the lough. History repeated itself in the early stages of the First World War when the threat then came from Germany, and, for a short period in 1914, the lough became the headquarters of the British Fleet. It is difficult today to reconcile the tranquil beauty of Lough Swilly with those turbulent and exciting times.

The archaeology of the lough awaits focused research but sufficient information currently exists to show that almost all phases of human occupation of Ireland over the last 10,000 years are represented around its shore. During this long period the lough has not been static, and considerable changes in relative sea level have taken place resulting in both submerged landscapes and raised sea beds and foreshores.

The entrance to Lough Swilly from the Atlantic Ocean is well defined by the two sentinel-like promontories of Fanad Head and Dunaff Head and within it the adjacent lands can be divided into three distinct regions – the Fanad Peninsula on the west, the Inishowen Peninsula on the east and between them, on the south, the lowland of the Lagan. These three natural divisions form discrete social units throughout history. The topography of the peninsulas also influenced the pattern of settlement, with the inhospitable central uplands having caused settlement to be focussed on the coastal rim. There is, in places, an extensive foreshore, a large area of which to the south of Inch Island has been lost to mid-nineteenth-century land reclamation.

The heritage of Lough Swilly (and of County Donegal) has been well served by a number of past and on-going initiatives on which this brief overview is based. The Ordnance Survey memoirs of the 1830s and Lacy's pioneering archaeological survey of the county commissioned by Donegal County Council and published in

1983, form a solid backbone for research. *The Donegal Annual*, published continuously since 1947 by County Donegal Historical Society, has resulted in an ever-increasing accumulation of knowledge and awareness of the past. The excellent Donegal County Museum in Letterkenny and the more specialist Inishowen Maritime Museum and Dunree Military Museum, among other local institutions, have ensured the past continues to be celebrated.

The Fishermen of the Mesolithic (9000–4000 BC)

The culture and time period of the first colonization of man in Ireland following deglaciation is called by archaeologists the Mesolithic (middle Stone Age). This is a very long period lasting approximately 5,000 years about which only the broad outline facts have been established. Future archaeological work in Lough Swilly has the potential to contribute much to knowledge of this period. On the basis of stone tools (lithics) this long span of time is divided into the Early Mesolithic and the Late Mesolithic. The Early Mesolithic, during which the first humans arrived in Ireland, commenced c.9,000 years before the present (BP) and lasted about 1,500 years. In terms of stone technology it is characterized by the use of small flint tools including extremely small worked flints (microliths) used to make composite tools. Environmentally, this phase is called the Boreal as the landscape was dominated by dense forests of hazel and Scots pine (like the modern day Taiga or Boreal forest of Canada and Russia) and interspersed with small lakes. Only a very restricted range of animals were present. There is no evidence for red deer for instance, an important food source for Mesolithic communities elsewhere. The only major meat animal was the wild pig or boar. Because of this, both marine and freshwater fish were a major food source with salmon and eels being of great seasonal importance. At present there are no known Early Mesolithic sites in the Lough Swilly area but many that were submerged by the rise in sea level may await discovery below the waters of the lough.

The Late Mesolithic, c.7,500 to c.5,500 BP, is characterized by a stone technology dominated by the production of large flint tools (macrolithic) in contrast to the early period. This seems to have been a particular Irish technology as it is only found here (and in the Isle of Man). There is much evidence for the exploitation of fish but added to this is the widespread exploitation of shellfish. During the period a marked climate change took place to wetter conditions (the Atlantic Climatic episode), which initiated the formation of bogs and the growth of deciduous forests with much alder, birch, oak, hazel and pine. At Dunaff Bay a Late Mesolithic flint-working site has been found on a raised beach and the good quality of the flint suggests that it was imported from the North Antrim coast. In recent years the lough has been subject to two pioneering Late Mesolithic projects: in 1995 Kimbal carried out the Lough Swilly Archaeological Survey (LSAS) based on fielding-walking a large area on the south-east; and in 2001 Professor Peter Woodman conducted the Inch Island Landscape Project. Both studies have produced abundant evidence for the presence of Late Mesolithic man in the region. Woodman excavated two early oyster middens (concentrations of discarded shells) on the eroding coastal edge in Baylet townland on the southern shore of Inch Island in 2001 and 2002. Although they were predominately of Neolithic age, some weathered Late Mesolithic flint and Mesolithic radiocarbon dates demonstrate that the rich oyster beds in the lough were being exploited during the period.

The Farmers of the Neolithic (4000–2000 BC)

The mechanisms that influenced the transition from a hunter-gatherer to a farming lifestyle ('the agricultural revolution') are unclear and one of the central questions still to be resolved is whether it involved the arrival of new people or whether indigenous Mesolithic people adopted new food supply methods from abroad. At present archaeologists, to a certain extent backed up by DNA information, favour the concept of continuity of the same people gradually adopting new farming technology and importing new animal and plant species from abroad. Neolithic culture entailed a radical change from earlier lifestyles. It involved a change to a settled farming way of life, clearance of the landscape for crops and pastures and its enclosure into fields, the use of pottery, and the building of impressive stone burial monuments (megaliths). The Lough Swilly region is rich in megalithic monuments of Neolithic society with at least 15 examples of court tombs, 5 of portal tombs, as well as a large number of unclassified sites. In contrast to the Mesolithic, when it seems people were concentrated on the coast, evidence demonstrates that in the Neolithic period people had spread all over the landscape.

The People of the Bronze Age (2000–400 BC)

Settlement during this 1600-year period is well represented in Lough Swilly. The evidence suggests that during the Bronze Age the region had a thriving and populous society. The period takes its name from the significant technological advance involving the extraction of copper ore and its alloying into bronze used to fashion tools (mainly weapons). Examples of all the main types of Bronze Age metal artefacts have been found around the lough – axes, swords, daggers, halberds and others. Megalithic burial monuments classified as 'wedge-tombs' were constructed at the beginning of the period for important members of society. There are seven good examples of these on both sides of the lough. Another burial tradition was the deposition of the remains in stone-lined cists (sometimes covered by stone cairns) and often accompanied by grave goods such as pottery and artefacts. A fine example of one of these, which contained perhaps twenty-five cists, was located in Killcolman townland near Rathmullan. Many of the numerous standing stones in the region may also date to the Bronze Age. A small number of cooking sites named *Fulachta Fiadh* by archaeologists have been found. In the region there are also a small number of ritual sites in the form of stone circles from the same period.

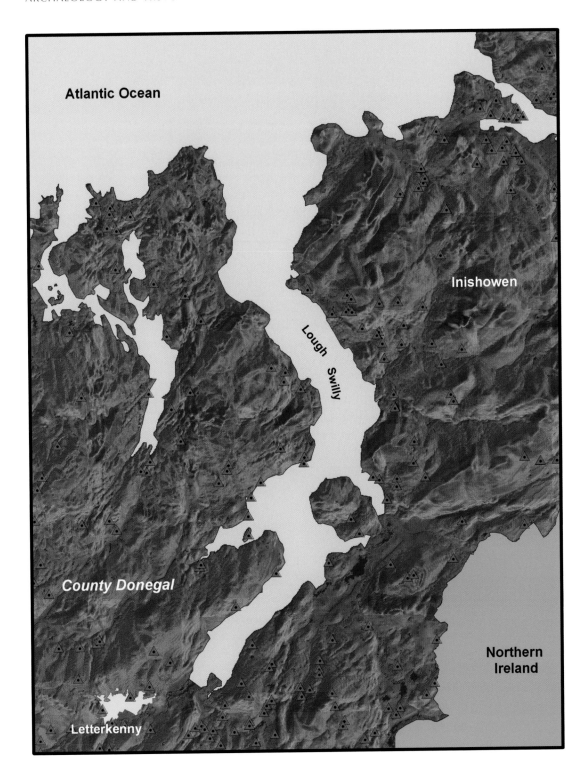

4.1 The Neolithic and Bronze Age sites of Lough Swilly: court tombs, portal tombs, wedge tombs, unclassified megaliths, stone circles, stone alignments, cairns, cists and standing stones.

The Warriors of the Iron Age (400 BC–AD 400)

This period saw the emergence of a warrior aristocracy with an increase in the use of swords and the construction of defensive earthworks known as hillforts. It is difficult to detect much archaeological evidence for this time period. However, crowning Greenan Mountain, commanding panoramic views over lough Foyle as well as Lough Swilly, is the hillfort called the Grianán of Aileach. The reconstructed stone-walled fort (cashel) is of Early Medieval date but it is surrounded by three outer enclosures (now largely invisible), which may date to the Iron Age or possibility to the Late Bronze Age. The site may have been used for ritual or ceremonial purposes rather than in a defensive role.

Early Medieval Society (AD 400–AD 1200)

In the fifth century Christianity reached Ireland and in the succeeding centuries became, through its churches, monasteries and culture, a dominant force in society. In this period it is possible, for the first time, to name peoples and communities who inhabited the landscape and the archaeological sites. The 'official' history of Donegal (recently re-evaluated by Dr Brian Lacey) tells of its conquest from the Ulaid (the Ulstermen) in the early fifth century by the four sons of Niall Noígíallach (Nial of the Nine Hostages), king of Tara – Conaill Gulban, Cairpre, Énna and Éoghan. They divided their new lands among them, with Conaill getting the lions' share of most of the south and west of the county including probably the western half of the lough. Éoghan got the peninsula named after him, Inishowen, while Énna got the area to the south of this (Tir Enna), which included the lands at the southern end of the lough (the modern Lagan). Inishowen was part of a large Cenél nEóghain over-kingdom called Aileach and it has been taken, somewhat for granted, named after the Grianán of Aileach. However, recent scholars suggest that the royal site from which the over-kingdom is named is a now-destroyed site in Elaghmore townland in County Derry.

Over the next 1,000 years the descendants of Conaill (the Cenél Conaill) and Éoghan (the Cenél nEóghain) dominate the history of the north-west and indeed, at times, made a major impact on Ireland as a whole. The written sources also document traces of other earlier peoples. Fanad may have been occupied by a tribe called the Corpraige and Inch Island by the Cuirenrigi, each of which had their own little kingdoms.

Early Medieval Ireland was dominated by great monasteries that controlled large segments of the landscape. The most important monastery around the lough was that of St Mura at Fahan, an early seventh-century foundation and chief monastery of the Cenél nEóghain. Today little is visible of this once-influential centre except for a very important decorated cross-slab known as St Mura's Cross of possible seventh-century date. The slab is decorated on both sides with crosses formed by interlace and displays very accomplished stone carving. The decoration is relatively unique in an Irish context and may display influences from Iona and

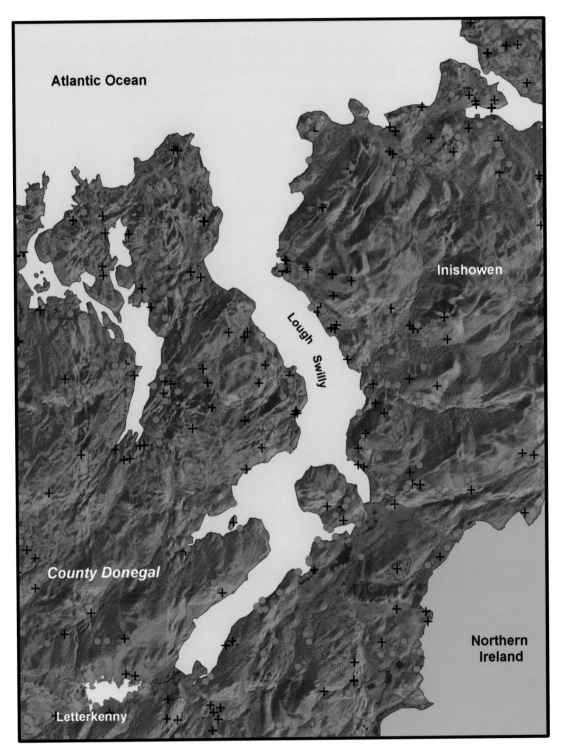

● Ringforts, earthworks, enclosures, promontory forts and souterrains

✚ Ecclesiastical sites, burial sites, holy wells and other sites with a religious association

4.2 The Early Medieval settlement landscape of Lough Swilly: ringforts, promontory forts (raths and cashels), souterrains and ecclesiastical sites.

4.3 St Mura's
cross-slab at Fahan.
Photo: Nigel McDowell.

from Northumbria. The Swilly region has some of the finest examples of cross-slabs in Ireland from the period, with Inishowen and Carndonagh being particularly distinguished. Another fine example can be seen at Drumhallagh, to the west of Macamish Point. Some of the sites of the early monasteries and churches continued in use in the Late Medieval period as parish churches or burial sites, and some are still in use today. Tidal islands provided an ideal spiritual location for many early monasteries, as they possessed an otherworldliness, being cut off for half of the day by the tide. The former church sites at Killygarvan Island (where Early Medieval burials have been found) and Aughnish Island, north and east of Ramelton, respectively, are fine examples.

Ringforts, in the form of circular or oval bank and ditch earthworks (raths), or drystone built enclosures (cashels), are the main known settlement form of the period. Examples abound around the lough demonstrating the presence of a populous and well-settled Early Medieval society. Dundrean, which gives its name to a townland near Bridgend, is a fine example of a bivallate (two bank form) of high status, and possibly royal ringfort. Another high status site type found in the area is the coastal promontory fort of which there are at least four known examples, and it seems likely in addition that underneath the nineteenth-century military fortification at Dunree Head there was one that gave the element *Dun* (Irish for fort) to the name of the headland. Examples of souterrains (artificial caves) either associated with ringforts, church sites or on their own, belong to the period and there are many examples in the area, including a number on Inch Island.

The ninth and tenth centuries witnessed the onslaught of the Vikings around the Irish coast and far inland. They were active in Lough Swilly and the archaeological and historical evidence, although slight, is quite significant. An entry for 921 in the Annals of Ulster mentions that a Viking fleet of 32 ships had abandoned a settlement at a place called *Cennríg*, tentatively identified as Dunree Head, and the corresponding entry in the Annals of the Four Masters (dated 819) mentions the arrival of a Viking fleet of 20 ships at Cenn Maghair (Kinnaweer) at the head of Mulroy Bay. Further evidence of Viking interaction in the Swilly area at this time is a concentration of Viking Age silver arm-ring hoards in north-west Inishowen that possibly date to the 920s or 930s. It is highly probable that a high degree of interaction existed between the Vikings and the local communities but it is doubtful if they were able to establish permanent settlements around the lough because of the power of the strong local kingdoms (the Cenél Conaill and Cenél nEóghain), who had their own fleets, allowing them to confront the maritime invaders both at sea and on land.

The Late Medieval Gaelic Lordships (1200–1607): the O'Donnells, MacSweeney Fanad and O'Doherty of Inishowen

During the late twelfth and thirteenth century the Swilly region remained relatively untouched by the Anglo-Norman settlement that penetrated much of Ireland. However, during the early fourteenth century, under the earl of Ulster parts of Inishowen came under Norman power, particularly after the building of the great castle of Greencastle on Lough Foyle. This short-term incursion has left little trace though, and it can be concluded that its effects on the ground were very superficial. Throughout the Late Medieval period, the O'Donnells (then current representatives of the ancient Cenél Conaill), exercised a very stable and strong lordship over Donegal (Tír Conaill). Much of their strength lay in the support of and control over five leading sub-lordships: the O'Boyles, the three MacSweeneys (Fanad, Doe and Banagh) and O'Dohertys. Four of these Gaelic lordships converged around the lough. In the west was MacSweeney Fanad, which encompassed the Fanad Peninsula, north of Ramelton and the Leannan River. To the south of this was a territory normally allotted to the *tanist* (recognized heir) to the

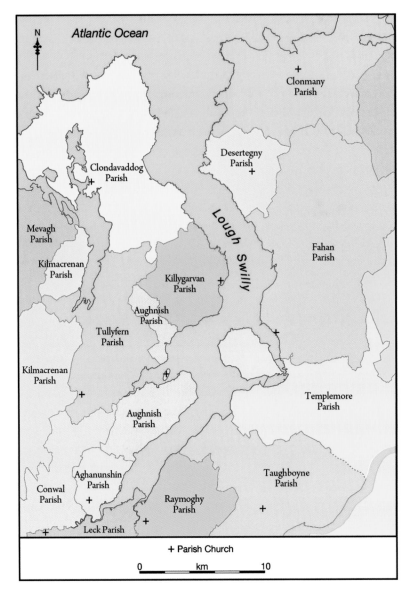

4.4 The Medieval parishes and parish churches around Lough Swilly.

current O'Donnell and was called in the late sixteenth century 'Hugh Duff's Country' or Clanelly. It extended from Ramelton to the Swilly River. The land around the southern margin of the lough and stretching from the Swilly River to Burt and much further to the south and west was held directly by the O'Donnell.

All of Inishowen, wrestled from the Cenél nEóghain and now under Cenél Conaill control, on the eastside of the lough, constituted the O'Doherty lordship. The first map showing these territories as distinct units, *Generalle Description of Ulster*, shows the major castles and some of the churches. It was compiled in 1602–3 near the end of Gaelic independence, while further important information is provided by a despatch in the state correspondence dated 1601 entitled 'The names of all the chief places of strength in O'Dogherty's country called Ennisowen, as well castles as forts; also of those in McSwyne Fanat's country'.

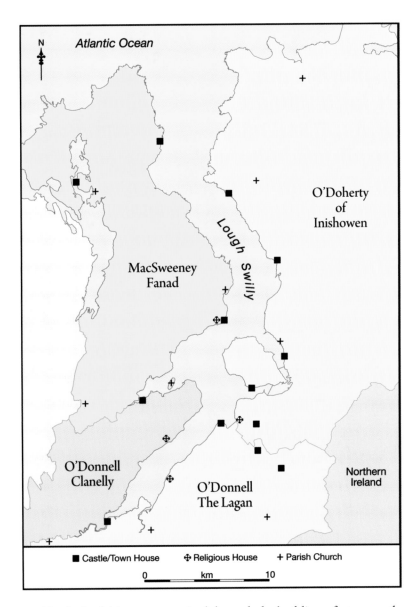

4.5 The Late Medieval landscape, the Gaelic lordships, castles/tower houses, parish churches and religious houses.

Control in the lordships was exercised through the building of stone castles and in the mid-fifteenth century Donegal, as elsewhere in Gaelic Ireland, went through a vigorous phase of castle building. Though conveniently referred to as castles, the vast majority of these were tower houses. The coastline of Lough Swilly was particularly fortified with castles at Moross, Doaghcrabbin, Rathmullan, Ramelton, Coolmacatraine near Newtowncunningham, Burt, Inch, Fahan and Buncrana. The location of castles within the region follows a very predictable pattern. Almost all are coastal, with some sited right on the coastal edge. Some are located in tidal river mouths and overlook good landing places or bridging points, with a view to controlling communications, and many are on the boundaries of their territories. Some are located at valuable salmon fishing places, as at Buncrana, Ramelton and

4.6 Killydonnell
Franciscan friary.
Photo: Nigel McDowell.

elsewhere. All the lordships around Lough Swilly had a strong maritime dimension
and used boats for military purposes as well as trade and communication.

Gaelic lordship was expressed in many ways, one of which was endowing
religious houses in order to provide spiritual and other cultural support for their
people, to enhance the prestige of the lordship and to provide a prestigious burial
place for their lineage. Three new religious houses were founded in the late
fifteenth or early sixteenth century around the lough. These were Rathmullan
Carmelite priory, and Killydonnell and Balleeghan Franciscan friaries.

During the twelfth century the church in Ireland (and throughout Western
Europe) was subject to radical reform. A central feature of the reform project was
the formalization of diocesan boundaries and the establishment of a fixed parish
framework. As the new dioceses were based on the political and territorial realities
of the twelfth century the Swilly region was split between the Derry diocese
(corresponding with the over-kingdom of the Cénel nÉoghain) and Raphoe
(corresponding to that of the Cénel Conaill). Thus Inis Eoghan (Inishowen), then
a Cénel nÉoghain territory, was assigned to the See of Derry, while the southern
and western portion of the lough, under Cénel Conaill control, was placed in
Raphoe. The first overview of the new parochial structure is provided by the Papal
Taxation lists of 1302–6 and it is clear that by the early fourteenth century, and
most probably considerably earlier, the parish layout around Lough Swilly was in
place. The lands around the lough were covered by twelve medieval parishes. They

4.7 Rathmullan Carmelite priory and Bishop Knox's manor house. Photo: Nigel McDowell.

are from north-west to north-east: Clondavaddog, Killygarvan, Tullyfern, Aughnish, Aghanunshin, Leck, Raymoghy, Taughboyne (includes modern All Saints), Templemore (includes modern Burt and Inch parishes), Fahan (now Upper and Lower), Desertegny and Clonmany.

The economy of the lordships rested on their agricultural produce, with cattle playing a major role. Their maritime setting meant that overseas trade was a significant part of the economy with the export of fish and the import of wine. All these lordships had close connection – through trade, intermarriage and general contact – with western Scotland. The Gaelic system of land organization and assessment divided the landscape into estates called ballybetaghs made up of townlands and the survival of the latter with their names form a very potent legacy of the medieval period. The medieval parishes also belong to this legacy, as they were used as the basis for the civil parishes and their framework was followed to a large degree by both the Church of Ireland and Catholic Churches. The end of the Gaelic lordships in Donegal began in earnest in May 1600 during the last stages of the Nine Years War, when Sir Henry Docwra landed in Derry after a voyage from Chester via Carrickfergus with a naval force of some 2,000 troops.

MacSweeney Fanad

By the twelfth century, if not considerably earlier, the O'Breslins, a branch of the Cénel Conaill, controlled Fanad, but by the fourteenth century they had been displaced by the MacSweeneys. This family were of Scottish origin with land in Knapdale in Argyll and were introduced to Ireland as mercenaries (gallowglass) in the early fourteenth century, and, while hiring themselves out to a number of Gaelic lords, they swiftly became an indispensable military force for the

4.8 The O'Doherty castle on Inch Island commands a strategic view up the lough. Photo: Andrew Cooper.

O'Donnells. In return for their services they acquired three sub-territories in the over-lordship: Fanad and Doe in north Donegal, and Banagh around Killybegs in south Donegal. Other branches of the family obtained lands through their role as gallowglass in Connacht and Kerry. MacSweeney Fanad was regarded as the senior branch and their lordship covered most of the Fanad Peninsula north of the River Leannan.

The MacSweeneys were a maritime people with their own fleet. They operated over a wide coastal area centred on the north and west coast of Ireland and the Scottish Isles. Their little territory is an interesting example of a Gaelic lordship in miniature. The centre of the lordship was Rathmullan where MacSweeney Fanad had his castle (of which nothing visible remains) on a rocky promontory on the coast. After the foundation of the Carmelite monastery in 1516 by Rory, the then-lord, and his wife, Mary O'Malley, Rathmullan also became the main religious and cultural centre of the lordship, and was the main port of Lough Swilly. There was another castle at Moross, and it is the only one in the lordship of which something remains. It was built in 1532 on the north-west border of the lordship on a promontory over Mulroy Bay that served as a ferry point. There was also a small castle at Doaghcrabbin overlooking the lough whose history is unknown. Apart from castles or tower houses there is little known about other secular buildings so it is of interest to note a reference in the *Calendar of the State Papers relating to Ireland for 1601* that one Walter McLaughlin MacSweeney lived in 'a little stone house' adjacent to Ramelton.

Rory, the lord of Fanad who died in 1518, and his wife Mary, are perhaps the most remarkable of the family. Mary, who was the daughter of O'Malley, lord of

4.9 The O'Doherty castle at Buncrana. Photo: Nigel McDowell.

another maritime lordship in County Mayo, was a pious and learned figure. She commissioned a work that has become known as the Book of Clan Sweeney (*Leabhar Clainne Suibne*, Royal Irish Academy Manuscript no. 475), which apart from its mainly religious content, contains some family history. One passage provides a rare glimpse of some of the social ritual within the lordship, recording that on Sunday the household of MacSweeney Fanad consisting of 150 men with wives and other women folk, musicians, poets and other servants went to mass in the parish church of Clondavaddog and that they laid, 'eight score hilted swords ornamented with gold and silver' on the altar.

Hugh MacHugh Duff's Country – Clanelly

The headquarters of this small lordship was at Ramelton on its northern boundary with Fanad, along the Leannan River. The castle, of which there are no visible remains, overlooked the tidal portion of river at the eastern end of the modern town. It was built by Neachtain O'Donnell, lord of Tir Connaill (1439–52), for one of his sons, MacAoidh, and in 1601 it was occupied by Hugh MacHugh Duff O'Donnell who, for a short time, had been the O'Donnell *tanist*. Clanelly (*Gleann Eighle*), according to an Inquisitition held at Lifford in 1603, contained thirty quarterlands. Killydonnell Franciscan friary (Third Order Regular), founded in 1471 on the site of an earlier church called Cill Ó dTomhrair, is the only substantial Late Medieval ruin to survive in this lordship.

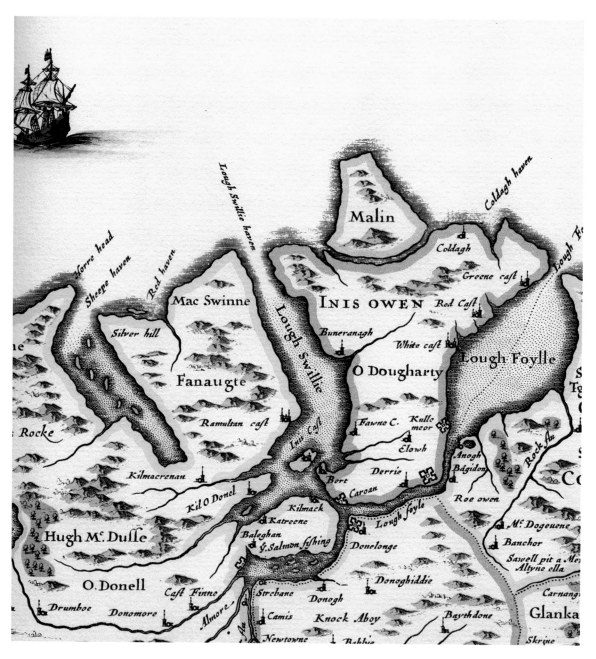

The map shows place names including: Horre head, Sheepe haven, Red haven, Lough Swillie haven, Coldagh haven, Malin, Coldagh, Greene caſt, Mac Swinne, INIS OWEN, Red Caſt, Silver hill, Buneranagh, White caſt, Lough Foylle, Fanaugte, O Dougharty, Rocke, Ramultan caſt, Fawne C., Kulle meor, Rock Au, Kilmacrenan, Elowh, Anogh, Bagidon, Kil O Donel, Bert, Derrie, Caroan, Roe owen, Kilmack, Lough Foyle, Hugh Mc. Duſſe, Katreene, Baleghan, Mc Dogeuene, Y. Salmon fiſhing, Donelonge, Banchor, Sawell pit a Me, Altyne ella, O. Donell, Caſt Finne, Donoghiddie, Carnang, Drumboe, Donomore, Almore, Strebane, Donogh, Baythdone, Glanka, Camis, Knock Aboy, Skrine, Newtowne

4.10 The Lough Swilly region in the map of Ulster in Blaeu's *Atlas Novus*, 1654, based on an earlier survey of *c*.1602–3. The map shows the perception of the Inishowen Peninsula as being an island cut off from the mainland along the Pennyburn depression. Malin is similarly, but also wrongly, depicted as a separate island.

The Lagan or Portlough

The area from the Swilly River eastwards to Burt was under the direct control of the O'Donnell lordship. This rich fertile area constituted the northern part of what became known in the seventeenth century as the Lagan. The main O'Donnell castle in the portion of this territory adjoining the lough was Culmactraine. There are no visible remains of this castle, first mentioned in 1456 in the Annals of the Four Masters. It was located in the Castleforward demesne to the east of Newtowncunningham and although it is now a considerable distance inland it was, before the mid-nineteenth-century reclamation of the horse-shore bay, now named Blanket Nook, quite close to the shore. On the north-west corner of this former bay in Drumboy townland, there was another castle site called Dunboy referenced in the *Calendar of the State Papers relating to Ireland of 1601*. Like Clanelly, this territory had also a Franciscan friary (Third Order Regular) at Balleeghan, of which there is substantial fifteenth-century remains; it is thought to have been founded, like Killydonnell across the lough, in 1471.

O'Doherty of Inishowen

Before the mid-nineteenth-century land reclamation Inishowen was almost an island connected to the rest of the country on the south by a narrow neck of land. Once the heartland of the Cenél nEóghain, by the fifteenth century it had come under Cenél Conaill control, when the O'Dohertys emerged as lords in the early fourteenth century replacing the MacLoughlins. Below the O'Dohertys in the lordship were a number of prominent families of freeholder status, the most notable of which were the McDaids or McDevitts (*Mac Daibhéid*) and the former rulers, the MacLoughlins. The O'Dohertys controlled their lordship through a string of castles located around the peninsula, the principal ones being Elagh and Burt, both situated on the southern boundary of the lordship. Burt, like Culmactraine nearby, has also lost through reclamation its landscape context immediately over-looking the lough. It is located on top of a prominent hill, originally almost an island being surrounded by the lough on three side. The remains of this castle are impressive and dominate the local landscape. Nearby, on the shore below the castle, are the ruins of a church on a grange (an outlying farm or estate) belonging to the Cistercian monastery of Macosquin to the south-west of Coleraine in County Derry. This little grange would have served as a fishing station and gave the monks a share in the rich fishing of the lough. The substantial ruins of the O'Doherty castle on Inch Island, first mentioned in 1456 (Annals of the Four Masters), are situated overlooking the shore on the south of the Island and near a ford across from the mainland. There was a tower house at Fahan, which belonged to the bishop of Derry. The O'Doherty tower house or castle at Buncrana is the best preserved of the Gaelic castles around the lough. It is situated overlooking the Crana River, a short distance from its mouth, and would have controlled the landing place on the adjacent shore, as well as the north–south land route on the peninsula.

The Plantation of the Seventeenth Century

Following their defeat in the Nine Years War (1594–1603) and the subsequent decline in their power, Rory O'Donnell, earl of Tyrconnell, Hugh O'Neill, earl of Tyrone, along with some others of the Gaelic nobility, boarded a French ship at Rathmullan on 14 September 1607 and sailed into exile in Europe where they hoped to rally Spanish support for their cause. Their aspirations were not fulfilled.

Symbolically at least, the 'Flight of the Earls' from Rathmullan heralded the end of Gaelic Ireland, and the imposition of a new social, political and economic order. The suppression of the Gaelic lordships and the confiscation of their land opened up the landscape for colonization and with the implementation of the Plantation scheme the land and shores around the lough emerged from the relative isolation of Gaelic culture into the new world order. While British colonization entailed a massive change in land holding and settlement forms, and introduced new people from England and Scotland, it is important to stress that in places around the lough a great continuity of Gaelic culture, people and landscape elements survived.

Initial planning for the scheme began in 1608 and by 1610 arrangements were in place for the granting of estates to the incoming colonizers. The lands in the former lordships were organized into 'precincts', which were subdivided into estates (called 'proportions') of three sizes: great (2,000 acres), middle (1,500 acres) and small (1,000 acres). These were to be formed into manors and to be granted to two classes of colonists, undertakers and servitors, along with a very small allocation to 'deserving natives'. The undertakers were obliged to build a defensive bawn (fortified courtyard), establish settlements and bring British tenants to their estates. The barony of Kilmacrenan, which included the Fanad Peninsula, was assigned to servitors and native Irish, while the precinct of Portlough was assigned to Scottish undertakers. A small portion of the precinct of Lifford, which extends to the south-west corner of the lough to the east of Letterkenny, was assigned to English undertakers. An exception to the general plantation model was made for Sir Arthur Chichester, the lord deputy, who was granted the entire barony of Inishowen in February 1609. Some land in the region was granted to Trinity College Dublin, while the ancient church or erenagh lands were confirmed to the bishops of Raphoe and Derry of the established church, and the land of the suppressed religious houses was granted away.

In Fanad, Rathmullan was granted to Sir Ralph Bingley but quickly passed to his son-in-law Bishop Knox. Some members of the MacSweeneys were granted small estates as 'deserving natives'. Rathmullan was incorporated as a town and house plots and lands were set aside for the inhabitants. In 1618 Knox modified the Carmelite friary into a manor house and it remained the residence of the Knox family until the late eighteenth century.

In the former Clanelly, Captain William Stewart (later knighted) of Whithorn in Wigtonshire, obtained an estate adjoining the lough and built a bawn or fort, the ruins of which still survive on the shore at Fort Stewart. A short time later he obtained an additional estate around Ramelton and Pynnar's survey reports that by 1619 he had made 'a large town' of 45 houses with 57 British families and a water mill, and was building a church. The early years of the plantation also witnesses the start of a town at Letterkenny, when in 1616 Sir George Marbury was granted a licence for a weekly market and two annual fairs.

Most of the land in Portlough precinct covering most of the southern portion of the lough was granted to three settlers called Cunningham from Ayrshire (to the south-east a further estate was granted to another Cunningham), who along with their lands, were granted free fishing in the lough. John Cunningham obtained land to the west of Burt and founded the developed the village of Newtowncunningham. To the west of this was the estate of James Cunningham who founded the village of Manorcunningham while to the east was that of Cuthbert Cunningham who appears to have not developed his holding and it was eventually absorbed into the estates of others. By Pynner's survey in 1618–19 John had built a house, a bawn and a village with twenty-six houses (Newtowncunningham) and a good mill while at the same date James had built his bawn but there is no mention of a village. Both settlers were granted weekly markets and two annual fairs.

In Inishowen, outside the formal Plantation project, Chichester had let out land to a number of settlers. Burt Castle was rebuilt with additions, as was Inch Castle, and their surrounding lands were let to colonists. Buncrana was leased to Captain Henry Vaughan who repaired the castle and developed the town, which had been granted a weekly market and two fairs annually.

While the Plantation made a massive change to the economy and society around the lough a strong stream of continuity with the late medieval Gaelic system survived. The major settlements of Rathmullan, Ramelton and Buncrana were all located around castles of the Gaelic lords and their associated clusters. While the Portlough or Lagan area was heavily settled by Scottish colonists, the bulk of Fanad and Inishowen remained overwhelming Gaelic, and indeed Irish-speaking down to the mid-nineteenth century. The Gaelic system of landscape organization was fossilized into modern townlands.

Landlord and Tenants in the Eighteenth and Nineteenth Centuries

The landscape of eighteenth- and nineteenth-century Ireland was strongly influenced by the landlords living in big houses and landed estates. Around Lough Swilly as elsewhere, the character of rural and town settlement was very much determined by the policy of estate management, or lack of it, within individual estates. In some areas improving landlords make a significant difference. The extremely picturesque views over the lough exerted many of the local landlords to site their 'big houses' with their parklands in lough-side locations and although many of the landlords were absentees, some of them built houses around the shore as bathing lodges and summer residences.

The main gentlemen's seats starting in the north-west are listed here. Greenfort was built by Captain Barton overlooking Ballymastocker, south-west of Portsalon in c.1810. Drumhalla House was built in 1789 by Dr Knox. Fort Royal, overlooking Kinnegar Strand, was built by Charles Wray in 1807 and later enlarged; it is now a hotel. The Lodge (now Rathmullan House), just north of Rathmullan, was built by Lieutenant-Colonel Knox of Prehen in 1820 on his estate, and, in 1832 it was bought by Narcissus Batt who had previously used Hollymount nearby as a bathing lodge. The Drum, or Drumalla House, at the north end of Killygarvan Bay, was built in 1789 by Dr Knox of Lifford. Glenalla near Rathmullan, seat of the Hart family, was built *c.*1810, but is now in ruins. The Stewarts acquired a mansion called Fort Stewart overlooking the lough at the ferry point in the later eighteenth century. Further down the coast were Arddrumman and Castlewray belonging to the Mansfield family and Castlegrove, in a similar loughside setting, was the home of the Grove family. Near Newtowncunningham, and on the site of Culmactraine castle, the Forward family built a mansion in the 1730s and laid out an extensive demesne including a large deer park. The property passed by inheritance to the earls of Wicklow and has since been demolished. In *c.*1716 Colonel George Vaughan built a very fine mansion near the old castle in Buncrana, and, in 1718, laid out the main street in the town. Further north, Captain Arthur Benson, in the 1720s, built a similar house to Buncrana Castle and named it Linsfort Castle.

At the opposite end of the social scale the bulk of the population lived in house clusters known as clachans. These vary in size from a few houses to very large concentrations of village portions. Clachans were intimately connected with a form of collective farming known as rundale, with land being held under joint leases by a group of families. Each family had a number of intermingled strips of arable land and grazed their animals in common in unenclosed pasture. Some of the largest clachans were to found in the poorer and remoter parts of the lough in the north-west and north-east. Good examples were Arryheernabin and Doagh Beg, south-west of Fanad Head, and Bunnaton More beside Knockalla coastguard station.

On the Inishowen side the clachans of Magherabane and Toneduff, both south-east of Dunree Head, were of great size; indeed the writer of the 1835 Ordnance Survey memoir for Desertegney, in which parish they are situated, states of Toneduff that it was 'the largest agricultural village he had yet seen'. By the early nineteenth century landlords throughout Ireland were making a concerted effort to suppress the rundale type of tenure and practice, as it was agriculturally and economically backward. By the 1830s in the Swilly region it had been eradicated on many estates. In Clondavaddog parish in northern Fanad, however, it was still strong and a large part of the landscape was unenclosed. One 'improving landlord' of the area had by this date made considerable progress in breaking up rundale and had placed many of his tenants into individual farms. In much of the Fanad and Inishowen peninsulas, however, it was very resilient, and in some places lasted to the twentieth century.

Conclusion

Lough Swilly has been occupied by humans for more than 9,000 years, all of them trying to make a living under changing circumstances. Each successive phase of human history has modified the lough and its surroundings and contributes to the contemporary cultural and natural landscape. The archaeological remains and historical records help us understand how things have changed and help to set today's lough and its people in context.

Chapter 5

The Maritime Heritage of Lough Swilly

Thomas McErlean

Introduction

Beyond the dramatic events in the lough's maritime history, outlined in the previous chapter, the archaeology of the lough also records the more mundane but equally fascinating story of man's interaction with the marine and coastal environment. On its most fundamental level much of this interaction is about how past human settlement around the Swilly exploited marine food resources. The lough supplied early man with a rich source of fish, shellfish and seaweed. The main fish catch were the seasonal herring and salmon but it had an additional wide range of fish species including cod and flounder. Shellfish also constituted an important food source, with the rich oyster beds of the lough being among the most prolific in the country. In addition, the massive shell banks exposed at low water around the lough's shores were eagerly exploited in the seventeenth and eighteenth centuries to lime the arable fields of the surrounding lands. In a similar manner the harvesting of seaweed provided rich manure that greatly increased potato yields. During the eighteenth century, however, the more profitable use of seaweed was to burn it to produce kelp (an impure form of soda or sodium carbonate), which was in great demand for the linen bleaching process, the manufacture of glass and soap making. Other maritime industries carried on around the lough in the past included salt making and also rabbit husbandry, the regions sand dune systems and islands providing ideal habitats to maintain large warrens for fur and meat.

Perhaps the main attribute of Lough Swilly, and one that made it of international importance, was its role as a sheltered and secure harbour astride the great trade routes of the North Atlantic. This led it to become one of the best-guarded and most heavily fortified harbours in Western Europe.

The Fisheries of Lough Swilly

FORESHORE FISHING WITH TIDAL FISH TRAPS

Much early fishing was concentrated on the foreshore using tidal fish traps. By this method, employed as far back as Mesolithic times, a rich harvest could be obtained twice a day on the ebb of the tide without ever having to enter a boat, cast a net or dip a rod. A small number of tidal fish traps have been discovered in recent years on the foreshore of the lough and the discovery of more is to be expected if focused inter-tidal surveys take place. Such a survey in Strangford Lough dramatically increased the known number of tidal fish traps, some dating to the seventh century AD. Discoveries to date in Lough Swilly include wooden fish traps in the foreshore adjacent to Fort Stewart, Carrowcashel and Killydonnell. At the latter are a number of related lines of very closely spaced post stumps on the lower shore, while at Carrowcashel a line of post stumps spaced at about 30cm apart have been noted and wooden stumps have also been observed at Fort Stewart. At these sites the stumps represent supports for wattle fences but no examples of surviving wattlework have been found. There is also evidence for the use of stone traps in the lough. A circular stone feature that may have functioned as a fish trap has been found on the Carrowcashel foreshore and another form, a square stone enclosure or 'fish pound' used on the lough foreshore in 1739, has been recorded. These features are currently assumed to be medieval in date but further research may demonstrate that they date from an earlier period.

SALMON FISHERIES

The three main rivers, the Leannan entering the lough at Ramelton, the Crana entering at Buncrana and the Swilly entering east of Letterkenny, all had, in the past, significant salmon fisheries. The Stewart family owned the Ramelton salmon fishery at the mouth of the Leannan from 1610 to 1958. Writing in 1726, Boat mentions that this fishery had the unusual distinction of being in season through the whole year. In the nineteenth century the salmon weir here stretched over the full width of the river with no provision being made for ascending salmon but after 1866 it was modified to comply with the legal requirement for gaps. Near the salmon weir there was also an eel weir. The Buncrana salmon fishery belonged to the Vaughan family from 1610 to 1763 and then descended to various heirs. In the nineteenth century the salmon weir crossed the mouth of the Crana just north of the castle. Early references to salmon fishing in the Swilly River are less plentiful but in 1849 a loop net was in use. In c.1830 stake nets for salmon fishing were introduced to Ireland from Scotland and by 1832 they were in use at Rathmullan and Linsford and later also at Buncrana and Ramelton.

THE LOUGH SWILLY HERRING FISHERY

In the eighteenth century the Lough Swilly herring fishery was regarded as one of the most valuable in the country and Arthur Young has provided a very full account of the fishery as it existed in 1776. At this period it was regarded as a winter fishery, beginning in the middle of October and ending about Christmas, in contrast, for example, to the Strangford Lough one, a summer fishery commencing in July and finishing at the end of September. This permitted twelve boats from Portaferry to go annually to Lough Swilly when their own season was over. In 1773 an ambitious commercial fishery station was established on Doon Point on Inch Island by one of the leading merchants of Derry, Robert Alexander. Young has provided considerable detail about the enterprise and states that by 1776 the construction of a large salting complex designed to cure 100,000 herring a day using some 10 tons of salt was nearing completion, the final cost of which was likely to be £500. The station would use a large workforce including 40 women, boys and girls to gut the fish and 5 coopers to make barrels. Among the buildings in the complex was a store for coarse salt capable of holding 150 to 200 tons and one with the same capacity for storing fine salt, a gutting house, a curing house, a packing house and a cooper's shop. In addition, there was extensive accommodation for the staff and storage for boats (of which there were 17 or 18) and nets. In 1774 Alexander had 2 sloops and a 100-ton brig serving the fishery. In that year he exported 650 barrels of herring to Antigua in his brig and used the two sloops to service the Irish coastal trade. In 1776 some 1,750 barrels were exported to the West Indies.

The station provided an outlet for all the herring boats of the lough (numbering about 500 in 1775) to sell their catch. The boats were built and owned by the farmers and others around the lough, and, while some owners fished themselves, it was more common to lease them. The average cost of a boat was £10. The normal practice was that five men would lease a boat on a sharing basis. In a normal season a boat caught 6,000 herring a night. The average price of the herring straight from the water on was 4s. 2d. per 1,000 and the main bulk of the catch was sold for home consumption, the rest being sold to the large number of merchant ships that came specially to the lough to purchase herring. The agricultural commentator Young states that in 1776 (the year of his visit) herring were so plentiful that there was enough for 'all the boats in Europe' and that the fishermen said that shoals were so dense that 'it was difficult to row through them'. In 1780 there were 130 'bounty' vessels at the fishery and some 1,708 tons of salt were used for curing. These figures rose in 1781 to 147 bounty vessels and 1,914 tons of salt.

To encourage the development of the Irish fisheries the government paid a subsidy (a bounty) of 20s. for every tonne of the ships weight. To qualify the vessel had to be decked and be between 20 to 100 tonnes. In 1783 there were some 1,000 boats with four oars used in Lough Swilly. In contradiction to Young's description of the Swilly herring fishery being a winter one, Newenham states that in 1784, the herrings came during the last week of June and left about the last week of September. It would seem, therefore, that in the intervening time, the shoals had changed their behaviour. The same source states that there was a great decline in the shoal after 1785. This is backed up by the Ordnance Survey memoirs of the 1830s, which record that the herring fishery had changed considerably and undergone a considerable decline compared with forty years previously. In the memoir for Clondavaddog parish, the remark is made that 'This once beautiful supply of providence has now nearly ceased on the north west of Ireland'. However, the same source documents that the herring fishery was still significant in local economy in the 1830s. For instance, it records that sometimes '200 men in 40 boats, go from the Rathmullan area to Fanad lighthouse and between Inch and Buncrana to fish for herring'.

Oysters

The lough has very favourable environmental conditions for the European oyster (*Ostrea edulis*) and the discovery of prehistoric oyster middens on Inch and other places demonstrate the existence of oyster beds, and their exploitation by man, over many thousands of years. The detection of ancient shell middens is increasing with on-going surveys and oyster middens have been recently observed in the eroding cliff edge at Whale Head, north-east of Ramelton, and on the coast at Aughinish Island and Rathmullan. The waters around Inch were the main centre for oyster exploitation in the past; indeed such was its prominence that it is called in the grant of the island to Sir Ralph Bingley in 1604 *Inche ne oystre* – 'Inch of the Oysters'. Oyster fisheries at Fahan and Buncrana are mentioned in Bishop Montgomery's survey in 1606. The Ordnance Survey memoirs of the 1830s state that the best oysters in the lough were dredged in the Farland channel between Inch and the mainland at Burt. The same source also records that Rathmullan was celebrated for small oysters, which were mainly sold in Derry.

A new phase for oyster exploitation around the British and Irish coastline was ushered in with the coming of the railways, permitting their exportation in relatively fresh condition to a much wider market and leading to the establishment of commercial oyster farms. William Hart, a younger son of a major Inishowen landholding family, set up the Lough Swilly Oyster Company with the financial backing of family and friends in 1868. His oyster farm was located on the coast adjacent to Fahan and initial projections suggested that a nursery stock of oysters could realize some £40,000 in three years. In 1868 the company laid down some 155,000 small oysters sourced from Lough Foyle, 8,000 from Lough Swilly as well as 10,000 from elsewhere. During 1869, however, the company experienced difficulties getting young oysters, as none were available from Lough Foyle. The initial optimism about the success of the venture proved unfounded, and by 1872 the company was in financial troubles. It was offered for sale but no buyer was forthcoming and the Lough Swilly Oyster Company ceased production.

In the 1870s there was growing concern about an observed decrease in the natural oyster stock in Britain and Ireland. The 'Report on Oyster Fisheries, 1876' recorded that in Lough Swilly in 1876 the oyster beds were becoming depleted, and a closing of the oyster banks and a ban on picking young oysters was proposed. Though Ireland's native oyster beds have suffered massive decline since the nineteenth century, by good fortune *Ostrea edulis* still survives in the zone from Ramelton down to the estuary of the Swilly.

Shell Banks

In the eighteenth and nineteenth century shells were an important resource for use as a soil fertilizer on the surrounding acid soils and the extensive shell banks in the lough were eagerly exploited. Young noted in 1776, that the normal practice was to apply 40 barrels of rotten shells per acre and that a barrel of shells for burning

5.1 The old ferry jetty at Fahan. Photo: Nigel McDowell.

into lime cost 3*d*. a ton. The Ordnance Survey memoirs mention that in the 1830s an area formerly called Allison's Bay and the Oak Bank in the channel to Letterkenny were a rich source of shell, and indeed that the Allison's Bay shell banks were so abundant that they were nicknamed 'the gold mines of Lough Swilly'.

Ports, Harbours, Landing Places and Lighthouses

All of Lough Swilly can be regarded as one gigantic harbour. Indeed, its role as a safe and secure haven off the North Atlantic resulted in its fortification during the Napoleonic wars of the early nineteenth century as a response to its possible use by a French invasion force. This was also the reason why the lough was used by the British Fleet during the First World War. Indeed as the Ordnance Survey memoirs note it was 'considered to be by naval men one of the best harbours in the British dominion' and 'Mariners allow it would afford anchorage to the whole British navy'. This being so, it is remarkable to observe that before the latter half of the nineteenth century few quays or piers were in existence in any of the numerous landing places around the lough. Even at the leading ports of Rathmullan and Buncrana (both regarded as the most secure anchorages within the lough), only very rudimentary landing facilities were in place. Ballyrain, on the tidal portion of

5.2 The nineteenth-century quay at Lehardan, north of Rathmullan. Photo: Nigel McDowell. Notice how the structure exploits the natural wall formed by the rock outcrop.

the Swilly River, developed as a miniscule port to service the merchants of Letterkenny from 1773. A small quay was made in the early nineteenth century. The few piers that existed were in connection with the ferry points at Fort Stewart, Farland Point and a number of other places. This unsatisfactory situation was the cause of frequent complaint but things improved after the middle of the century when generous grants became available for the provision of harbour and pier construction from the Office of Public Works. A small pier built at Buncrana c.1850 was superseded by the much larger present structure in 1874. The fine piers at Kerr's Bay in Rathmullan and at Portsalon (extended in 1888–91), Leannan and Inch are of similar date. A wooden pier was made at Farland Point as a terminus for the steamboat ferry service to Rathmullan and Portsalon. In 1868 the terminus was moved to Fahan and the wooden pier was moved and re-erected there. Today the skeletal framework of the old wooden pier survives as a nostalgic and conspicuous feature on the foreshore.

At the beginning of the nineteenth century there were no lighthouses in Lough Swilly but the wrecking of the *Saldanha* in 1811 increased the demand for the provision of lights. This resulted in the building of a lighthouse on top of the cliff at Fanad Head at the entrance to the lough in 1817 (rebuilt in 1886). In 1876 it was joined by one at Dunree and another at Buncrana pier.

Fords and Ferries

5.3 Fanad lighthouse
Photo: Nigel McDowell.

Historically, the most important ford in Lough Swilly crossed the tidal reaches of the Swilly River about two miles east of Letterkenny. In the historical sources it was known as *Farsat Swilly* or *the Farsat of Soloughmore* and is now represented by the townland of Farsetmore on the southern bank of the lough about three miles west of Manorcunningham. The element farset in the name suggests that this ford, like many others, was based on a tidal sandbank across the foreshore. In 1098 the Annals of Ulster record that the Cenél Conaill were victorious over the Cenél nEóghain at a battle at *Fersad-Suilidhe*. The Annals of the Four Masters record that the ford was the setting for a great victory of O'Donnell over O'Neill on 8 May 1567. The O'Neill (Shane the Proud), in a military incursion into Tír Chonaill, had proceeded to the ford to do battle with O'Donnell who was at *Ard-an-ghaire* (modern Ardhee townland) on the other side of the estuary. The large O'Neill forces crossed over the ford and defeated a small O'Donnell cavalry force. Shortly after the main O'Donnell army arrived (largely consisting of the three branches of the MacSweeneys, Fanad, Banagh and na-dTuadh) and, in spite of their very much smaller numbers, succeeded in driving the enemy force back across the ford during a rising tide and many were drowned. The annals estimate O'Neill losses to be

5.4 The memorial cross in Fahan graveyard marking the mass grave of many of the crew of the *Laurentic*, which sank on 25 January 1917. Photo: Nigel McDowell.

from 1,300 to 3,000 men. The ford is also mentioned in a list of castles of the region compiled in 1602 that notes a fort in connection with the ford: 'there is a ford pasable at low water, wherein hath sometimes been a fort called the Farcet of Soloughmore'.

In the seventeenth, eighteenth and nineteenth centuries fords and ferries were of great importance and were normally privately owned and a source of revenue. The principal ferry in the lough in the eighteenth and early nineteenth century was between Fort Stewart and Ballybegley, a distance of one mile, and connected Ramelton to Newtowncunningham and on to Derry. The impressive tidal causeways and adjoining quays on both sides of this ferry are still extant. The other principal ferry in the lough was from Rathmullan to Inch Island and Fahan. Inch had, before the construction of the causeway from the mainland, two ferry connections – one from Quigley's Point on the east and one from Farland Point in the south.

Lough Swilly Wrecks

Lough Swilly's position on the North Atlantic shipping route, once one of the busiest in the world, and its role as a harbour of refuge to be headed to during difficult weather at sea, resulted in it having more than its fair share of shipping casualties. Maritime records reveal approximately 62 wrecking incidents within the lough or a short distance from its mouth over the last three centuries. Approximately three-quarters of these belong to the nineteenth century when shipping traffic was at its height. The corpus of wrecks includes a wide variety of nineteenth-century boat types, including battleships, brigs, barques, schooners, cutters, trawlers, steamers, tugs, smacks and ketches. The casualities encompass vessels en route to, or on return from, the Clyde, Liverpool, London, Scandinavia, St Johns and Quebec, New York, the West Indies and many other places. Local Irish coastal shipping also contributes a significant percentage and the list includes a small, but prominent, number of First World War casualities. Among the cargoes carried by the wrecked vessels, coal and grain predominate, while others were loaded with timber, granite and kelp and quite a few were carrying only ballast. In terms of cargo, however, it is the *Laurentic* (see below) with its load of gold bullion that captures the imagination.

Extreme weather conditions, catching fire and enemy action were the main causes of wrecking. One of the main hazards was the Swilly Rocks near the entrance to the lough on the north-west, which has claimed at least seven known victims but probably many more whose details are unknown. The sea around Dunaff Head has also claimed a significant number. At both locations many of the ships were heading to the lough for shelter. Strandings account for quite a number on the list, with ships being driven onto the shore at Fahan, Buncrana and

5.5 The bell of the *Laurentic* at Portsalon church. Photo: Nigel McDowell.

Inch Island. In these cases it was normally possible to retrieve much of the cargo and salvage some of the ship. The location of only a small number of the lough's wrecks have been precisely ascertained and research in progress hopefully will pinpoint more. This is a matter of some urgency as this superb heritage resource is in danger of being pillaged.

The two wrecks whose memory is enshrined in local folklore are those of the *Saldanha* in 1811 and the *Laurentic* in 1917. The *Saldanha*, a Royal Navy frigate of 38 guns and a crew of about 300 men, was driven by a north-west gale on to rocks off Ballymastocker Bay on the night of 4 December 1811. Wreckage including pieces marked *Saldanha* littered Ballymastocker Strand and accounts state that more than 200 bodies were washed in. The most prominent among the drowned was Captain William Packenham, son of the earl of Longford and brother-in-law of the duke of Wellington. Packenham was buried the following Saturday in Rathmullan. Eyewitness accounts describe that the local populace, as was customary, were quick to salvage anything of value for themselves, in spite of attempts by the locally-stationed Lanark militia to maintain law and order. The only survivor was the ship's parrot, captured a few months later near the site of the wreck and identified by a medallion around its neck engraved with the name

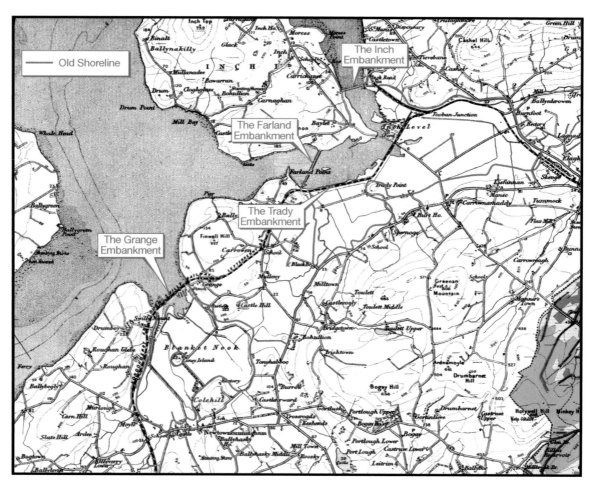

5.6 Land reclamation, 1840–59.

Saldanha. The place name Saldanha Head at the south end of Ballymastocker Bay commemorates this great naval tragedy.

The armed merchant cruiser, the *Laurentic*, was lost on 26 January 1917, sank by torpedo at the mouth of the lough with the loss of 350 of her crew, 68 of whom are buried in a mass grave in the Church of Ireland graveyard in Fahan. The *Laurentic* was carrying 3,211 gold bars with an estimated worth (today) of £300 million. Between 1917 and 1924, 3,168 of the gold bars were recovered. The wreck lies in about 40m of water, approximately two miles north of the lough. Its bell is in Portsalon church and some of its guns have been raised in recent years.

Reclamation

The extensive foreshore around the lough encouraged small-scale reclamation schemes from an early date. In the early nineteenth century an area of foreshore north of Manorcunningham was converted to farmland. Reclamation work in 1833 was carried out on part of the shore adjoining the townlands of Ardnaree and High Cairne, north-east of Ramelton, by the local landlords, the Stewarts, under the supervision of a Scottish engineer. A reclamation bank some 30ft to 40ft thick and from 10ft to 14ft high and 1,190ft in length constructed at a cost of £400 created a considerable number of acres of land. Today, lack of maintenance of the bank has resulted in renewed tidal submergence of the fields.

The greatest human modification and transformation of the lough took place between 1840 and 1859 when over 5,000 acres of foreshore were reclaimed in two shallow bays in the Burt–Inch area at a cost in the region of £280,000. This great project had a long gestation period and grew out of a proposed scheme formulated in the mid-eighteenth century to connect Lough Foyle and Lough Swilly by a canal through the narrow gap of the Pennyburn–Burnfoot depression. The Irish House of Commons was petitioned for funding in 1763 and again in 1765 but nothing came of it. The scheme was revived without success in 1807. More concrete steps were taken in 1831 when the great naval engineer Sir John Rennie was commissioned to prepare plans and costings and a figure of around £38,000 was suggested. The canal idea was dropped but in its place a reclamation scheme was proposed in 1836. This met with a favourable reception as a potentially profitable enterprise. The scheme was backed by a number of London investors and the necessary Public Act was passed in 1838 with the proviso that the work should be completed in ten years. Work commenced c.1840 and such was the scale of the project it was not completed until 1859, an extension to the original time limit being obtained by an Act passed in 1853. The sea was excluded by the construction of four major embankments and the former foreshore was formed into the townlands of Burt (Intake), Inch (Intake) and Blanket Nook (Intake). The major embankments are:

1. The Trady Embankment, which extended from Tooban junction to Farland Point. It was completed in 1850 at a cost of £80,000.
2. The Inch Embankment, which crosses from Inch Island to Quigley's Point on the mainland. It was completed in 1855.
3. The Farland Embankment, which extends across from Inch Island to just east of Farland Point. It was completed in 1856.
4. The Grange Embankment, which extends from the Grange of Burt to Blanket Nook. It was completed in 1859.

After completion the entire new intake was initially managed as one large agricultural unit, but after 1877 it was divided into individual leasehold farms. Around 1868 a brickworks using the glacial and marine clays of the former foreshore was established at Burnfoot by Messrs Wagstaff and Brassey, the owners of the reclamation lands in the area. In Derry, many houses were built with Burnfoot bricks. Unfortunately, they acquired a poor reputation because of their porous nature and the brickworks closed about 1920.

5.7 View from Inch showing
some of the reclamation banks.
Photo: Emmett Johnston.

Kelp Making

The harvesting of seaweed for kelp production was carried out on a large scale around the shores of the lough in the eighteenth and early nineteenth centuries. During the height of the industry the collection of seaweed to make kelp took precedence over its use as a fertilizer as it was extremely profitable for both landlord and tenant, the latter often paying their rent in money made from kelp making. As seaweed only grows on rocky shores considerable effort was made to extend its natural range by placing stones on muddy and sandy foreshores to form stone grids. These were quickly colonized by seaweed, which was then harvested on a rotational basis like an arable crop. Excellent examples of kelp grids can be observed at various locations, but especially along the wide inter-tidal zone on the south-western side of the lough from Whale Head southwards and on the opposite shore. A particularly good example can be seen at the Fort Stewart ferry.

One of the main industrial uses of Irish kelp was as an agent in the linen bleaching process and most of the Swilly kelp was bought by the local linen bleachers, the area being a major linen producing area with large bleach greens at Buncrana, Ramelton and elsewhere. With the virtual demise of this industry, however, the local demand for kelp ceased. The Ordnance Survey memoirs for the region, compiled in the 1830s, a few years after the industry had gone into steep decline, record some areas where it was still practised. At this date kelp continued to be made on the Atlantic shore at the northern end of the Fanad Peninsula in

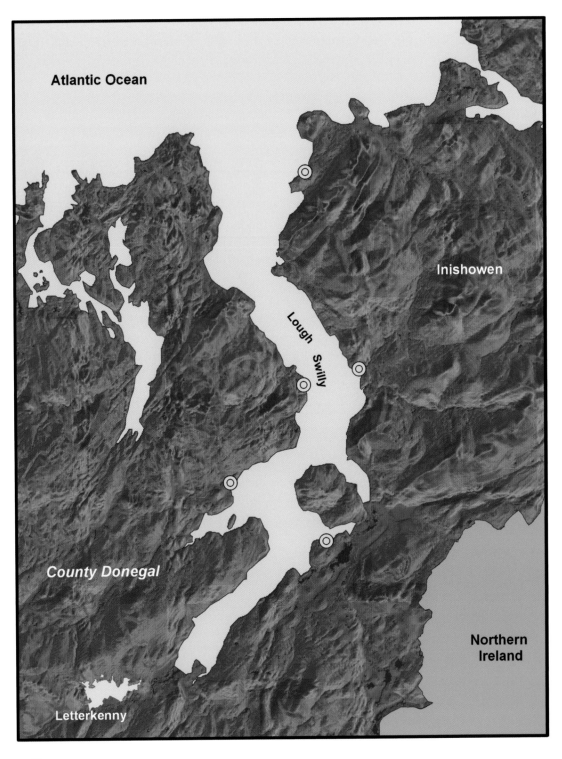

Salt manufacture

5.8 The location of salt pan sites of Lough Swilly.

Clondavaddog parish and was sold at £3 per tonne and exported to Scotland. Production had ceased in most of the parishes around the lough though. In the latter part of the nineteenth century some revival in the commercial harvesting of seaweed took place when it was used for iodine production, most of which went to Bond's Iodine factory in Buncrana, until its closure in 1900.

Salt Manufacture

During the eighteenth century salt production was a considerable industry around the lough. The availability of cheaper coal and improved shipping in the mid-eighteenth century encouraged a great increase in salt manufacture around the Irish coast. The main use for the locally produced salt was for curing fish, most notably the herring catch. The industry was not based on the evaporation of brine but on the import of rock salt from Chester and other places that was then refined into a purified form. Salt making in the lough has left little documentary evidence but its widespread practice can be traced at various locations. On the north-west, at about half a mile south of Macamish Point, the OS six-inch map (sheet 28) marks the buildings of the 'old salt pans' a short distance from the shore. These works gave their name to the surrounding townland of Saltpans and the little inlet on which they were situated was called Saltpans Bay. The OS map also marks the buildings of the salt works near the shore just south of Ray Bridge with the designation 'Saltings'. On the south of the lough there were salt pans beside the shore in Ballymoney townland to the west of Farland Point and opposite Inch Island. On the eastern side of the lough there was a salt works at Buncrana pier and before the construction of the latter the location was known as 'Salt Pan Point'. On the north-east of the lough on the shore of Leannan townland and north-east of Leanan Point was another salt pan. The location of all these works share the common features of being close to the shore and at landing places suitable for the landing of rock salt and coal. With the abolition of the salt duties in the 1820s the Lough Swilly industry collapsed. By 1823–4 the only working salt works in the lough was the one at Ray belonging to a Mr Watt; by the early 1830s this too had closed and its buildings were falling into decay.

Rabbit Warrens

The Anglo-Normans introduced the rabbit to Ireland in the late twelfth century as a domestic animal to be farmed for food and fur. During the Late Medieval period the ideal habitat for rabbit warrens were coastal sand dunes and islands. An early reference to a warren in Lough Swilly is to be found in Carew's survey of the progress of the Plantation in 1611, where in Buncrana Captain Henry Vaughan had made, among other improvements, 'a waaren well stored w'th conys'. This may have been the extensive warren that existed until comparatively recently in the sand dunes of the White Strand, to the south of Buncrana in Ballymacnarry townland.

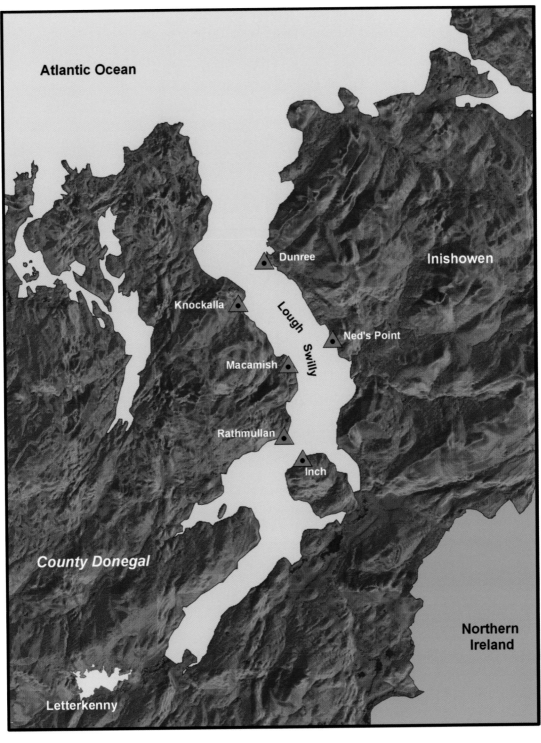

 Lough Swilly forts

5.9 The Lough Swilly forts.

5.10 Fort Dunree.
Photo: Emmett Johnston.

Evidence of rabbit husbandry once practised in the Lough Swilly area is provided by the place name Kinnegar (from *Coneygarth*), a townland of fifty acres in Killygarvan parish with its associated Kinnegar Strand and Kinnegar Point. Other place names include Coney Island, west of Burt. On the northern open coast there was an extensive warren in the sand dunes at Ballyhiernan Bay.

The Fortification of Lough Swilly

During the 1790s fear of a French naval invasion of Ireland intensified. This fear became a reality in December 1796 when a French fleet of more than forty ships and a force of some 14,000 men set sail from Brest, headed for Bantry Bay, under the command of General Lazare Hoche. Gale force winds prevented landing and the planned invasion was abandoned. During the 1798 rebellion another attempt was made. On 16 September 1798 a French squadron, probably heading for Lough Swilly, set sail. It was composed of a flagship, the *Hoche*, eight frigates and a schooner, and had 3,000 soldiers and the United Irish leader Wolfe Tone on board. On 11 October, however, the French squadron was defeated by a superior Royal Navy force off Donegal and the *Hoche* and six of the frigates, as well as Wolfe Tone himself, were captured and taken to Lough Swilly. The immediate response

5.11 Drumhalla Fort looking east. Photo: Nigel McDowell.

to the French invasion attempt was to erect temporary batteries at Lough Swilly and Bantry Bay. In Lough Swilly these batteries were located at Rathmullan, Macamish and Knockalla on the western side of the lough, and at Inch, Saltpans Hills, Ned's Point, Fahan Point, Lisfannan Point and Dunree Head on the eastern side. All these were in place by late 1798 or early 1799 and some of the captured guns from the *Hoche*, including eight 42-pounders, were immediately put to use as part of the new defence system.

After a short period of relative peace the French threat resurfaced in 1803–5 and work constructing coastal defences in Lough Swilly resumed. In 1804, naval signal stations with accommodation for a military guard were placed at Fanad Head and Malin Head, and gun boats were placed in the lough.

The intensification of the Napoleonic threat after 1811 lead to the construction of major defensive works in the lough during 1812–13. Six major forts (all on the sites of the earlier ones) were built, three on west side of the lough and three on the east side. The design for the defence of the lough was simple. Crossfire fields of twined pairs of forts on each side of the lough could effectively defend against any attempted landing by a naval force. Thus a fort at Knockalla on the west matched Dunree on the east, and one at Macamish matched Ned's Point, and Rathmullan matched Inch. Knockalla is situated on a cliff edge and is now a private residence. Dunree is situated on top of a high promontory and has been restored in recent years, and now houses a museum concerned with the Lough Swilly defences. Macamish has a Martello tower, a battery and powder magazine and is

5.12 Part of the British North Atlantic Fleet in Lough Swilly viewed from Rathmullan pier. Courtesy of the National Library of Ireland.

now a holiday residence. Its matching fort at Ned's Point, about two miles across the lough, is located on a rocky headland about a mile north-west of Buncrana and has been recently conserved. The battery at Rathmullan, now restored, was largely built in 1813 on the site of the temporary battery built earlier, and consists of a large masonry battery with a blockhouse and powder magazines. Inch Fort (now in ruins), a mile away across the lough, appears also to have been built in 1813, although a stone on it gives the date of 1815.

During the nineteenth century all the forts underwent various modifications but by the end of the century a major reconsideration of the Lough Swilly defences took place. The availability of guns of much greater range resulted in the abandonment of the matching forts system. In 1894 a scheme was adopted to concentrate on the eastern forts of Dunree, Ned's Point and Inch, which were improved, and to construct a new battery at Leannan Head, and decommission the three forts on the western side of the lough. In addition, a new fort was constructed further inland from Dunree (Dunree Hill Battery). Further modification followed and by 1914 Ned's Point and Inch were decommissioned, leaving only Dunree and Leannan. During the First World War Lough Swilly remained an important fortified Royal Naval base with the Navy's headquarters in Buncrana. It had an important role in protecting American merchant shipping passing the north coast.

Under the terms of the Anglo-Irish Treaty of December 1921 Lough Swilly, along with Cork Harbour and Bantry Bay, were retained by Britain and were to become known as the Treaty Ports, described by Churchill as 'sentinel towers of

5.13 Early twentieth-century view of the resort of Rathmullan showing the Pier Hotel. Courtesy of the National Library of Ireland.

the western approaches'. Lough Swilly was of critical importance as the base for protecting access to the Mersey and the Clyde. Dunree and Leannan continued to be garrisoned by British forces until the Anglo-Irish Treaty of 1938 when they were handed over to the Irish government. The handover of Dunree and Leannan took place with suitable ceremony on 3 October 1938. During the Second World War the Irish government carried out measures to update the remaining Lough Swilly defences. In 1940 three anti-aircraft positions were built at Dunree Hill Fort. In 1952 Dunree and Leannan ceased to have regular garrisons, apart from a small maintenance staff at Dunree.

Five of the six Napoleonic-period forts on Lough Swilly are in good repair and are well-maintained; the sixth, Inch, though ruinous, is also in relatively good condition. Collectively they constitute remarkable and impressive maritime monuments.

Resorts

From the early nineteenth century coastal settlement around Britain and Ireland was transformed by the rise of the resort industry. The fashion for sea bathing and visiting fashionable watering places increased throughout the century. Lough Swilly, though possessing all the natural attributes to make it a desirable location, lagged behind other parts of the Irish coast in developing a significant resort industry. Indeed the 1830s Ordnance Survey memoirs commented in reference to Rathmullan that it would 'possess far greater advantages than any other bathing places in the north of Ireland, Portstewart excepted' if it were to be developed as such. In the 1860s a number of developments came together that transformed the lough into a popular destination for visitors. One was the provision of the steamboat ferry service to Rathmullan and Portsalon (originally from Farland

LOUGH SWILLY HOTEL BUNCRANA 4499 W L

5.14 Early twentieth-century view from Buncrana pier showing Lough Swilly Hotel. Courtesy of the National Library of Ireland.

Point and later from Fahan), and the other was the construction of the narrow gauge Londonderry and Lough Swilly Railway (L&LSR) in 1863. The railway ran from Derry to Farland Point, but, in 1864, a line to Fahan and Buncrana was made and later extended to Letterkenny and further afield. Buncrana fast became a fashionable resort, especially for the inhabitants of Derry. In 1865 the Lough Swilly Hotel (built at a cost of £3,000) opened and numerous other boarding houses followed. In 1891 the golf links opened in the sand dunes at Lisfannon and other features of resort infrastructure were developed. At Portsalon the earl of Leitrim built a hotel and in 1891, the same year as Buncrana, golf links were created in the dunes behind Ballymastocker Strand. Similar developments took place at Rathmullan and Ramelton.

Conclusion

Lough Swilly has a rich and varied maritime heritage influenced by both external and internal forces. The exploitation of its resources has changed much over the passage of time. Early human exploitation of its shellfish and fish was joined by new methods of food production and capture, such as the establishment of rabbit warrens. Changing tastes in food and heavy exploitation continue to influence how the natural resources are used. Changing social and economic influences saw large areas of foreshore transformed into agricultural land in the eighteenth and nineteenth centuries. That land remains in agricultural production, but other industries like kelp and salt manufacture, that must have seemed innovative at the time, have come and gone. The importance of the lough for navigation has changed with time and, associated with this, its strategic role in geopolitics has waxed and waned. The advent of coastal resorts in the nineteenth century heralded a new type of exploitation through tourism that has resulted in many changes.

Chapter 6

The People of Lough Swilly

Loretta McNicholas and Rosita McFadden

Introduction

Humans have been drawn to Lough Swilly's resources since the first people set foot in Ireland (see Chapters 4 and 5). Since then they have left their mark on the landscape in many different ways and the modern landscape is very much a mixed cultural and natural one. This chapter is concerned with the people who currently live around the lough, the settlements they live in, what they do, their lifestyle and the challenges they face. The Swilly is, of course, also used by visitors for a variety of purposes, particularly recreation, the subject of Chapter 10.

The definition of the Lough Swilly catchment area in this chapter is based on the Electoral Divisions that bound Lough Swilly and those that follow the course of the Swilly river. From this perspective, the administrative catchment area comprises 22 Electoral Divisions[1], covering an area of 483.1 km^2 stretching over both the Letterkenny and Inishowen Electoral Areas

Although geographically the catchment area only represents approximately 10% of the land area of County Donegal, the major population centres of Letterkenny and Buncrana account for the relatively high population density in the area. The total population of the catchment area is 36,924, which is 25%[2] of the entire population of County Donegal, according to the 2006 Census.

The settlement structure in and around the lough is characterized by the coexistence of areas that are quite rural in nature (especially around the Fanad Peninsula and north-western Inishowen), in tandem with two of the largest urban centres in the county. The rural areas, in particular, are categorized as being quite isolated.

Settlement Patterns around the Lough

Thirteen towns speckle the land on the sides of the estuary. These towns can either be described as a census town[3], a control point town[4] or in some cases both.

---

1 Electoral Divisions (EDs) are the smallest legally defined administrative areas for which Small Area Population Statistics (SAPS) are published from the Census, CSO 2010.   2 Total population of County Donegal according to 2006 Census of Population was 147,264.   3 A census town, according to the CSO, is classified as a town with 50 or more households.   4 Control points are defined in the Donegal County Development Plan 2006–12 (as Varied) as the spatial demarcations of the towns and villages within the settlement hierarchy of the county, and delineate for policy purposes between urban and rural environments.

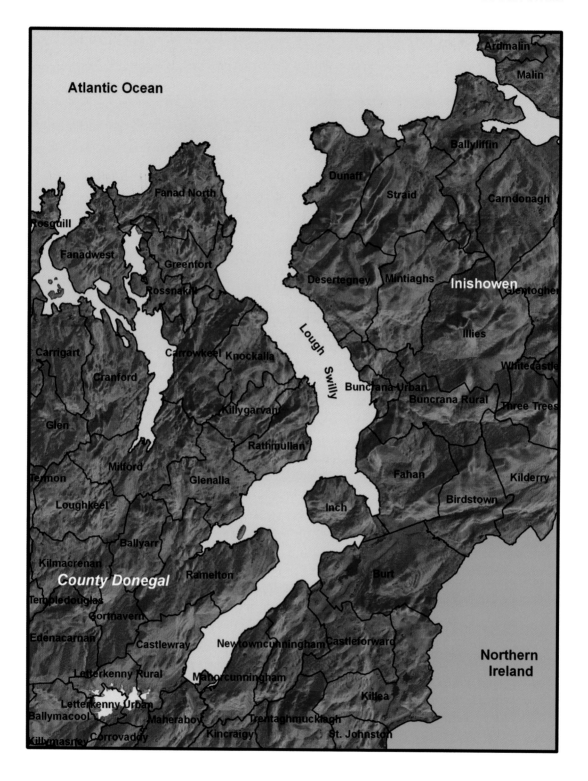

6.1 Map showing the Swilly 'administrative catchment area' based on electoral divisions that impinge on the Lough and River Swilly.

PROFILE OF THE TOWNS

Travelling from the Fanad Peninsula along the western side of the Lough, down the base of the estuary and then to Inishowen on the eastern side, the first town is Portsalon. This coastal town commands a prominent location at the entrance to the Lough Swilly Estuary and benefits from spectacular scenery. The town is a very popular tourist resort, with the Portsalon golf course paralleling the shores of the breathtaking Ballymastocker Bay, once voted the second-most beautiful beach in the world.

The next town is Glenvar, which is situated in the central part of the Fanad Peninsula and nestled below the Knockalla Mountains. Glenvar, the smallest town within the Lough Swilly catchment area, is conveniently located to Kerrykeel and Portsalon.

Bounded to the west by Mulroy Bay and lying in the shadows of the Knockalla Mountains to the north and Ranny Hill to the south, Kerrykeel makes an ideal base for touring the Fanad Peninsula and is within a forty-minute drive from Letterkenny.

Rathmullan, located on the western shores of Lough Swilly, is of renowned historical importance. Today sailing and fishing are among the main outdoor activities, with a regatta and a deep-sea fishing festival held in Rathmullan annually. The Inishowen Peninsula can be accessed from Rathmullan by ferry during the summer months.

As a designated heritage town, Ramelton is situated at the mouth of the Leannan River, which flows into Lough Swilly. The river forms a striking visual feature, along with the old warehouses, quays and the Georgian streetscape. Ramelton is the third-largest town in the Swilly catchment area and views of the lough can be enjoyed from the Town Park.

At the southernmost point of the lough is Letterkenny, the main commercial, retail and population centre of County Donegal. The town itself is situated on hillsides overlooking the Swilly. The town boundaries have sprawled in recent years to accommodate new residential developments and industrial units for many multi-national companies in its hinterlands, while the town centre has expanded greatly with many high street stores and commercial units being developed there. The cathedral town is steeped in history. Letterkenny plays host to many events, including the Donegal International Rally, the Earagail Arts Festival, the Pan-Celtic Festival and An Oireachtais and also offers many sporting and recreational pursuits, including GAA, soccer, athletics and golf.

Travelling north on the eastern shore, the first settlement encountered is Manorcunningham, which has experienced a 30% increase in its population from 2002 to 2006, possibly acting as a commuter town to Letterkenny, just 7km away. The small town is located along the N13 national primary road between Letterkenny and Derry. Manorcunningham has a very active community sector.

Newtowncunningham now acts mainly as a commuter town to serve both Letterkenny and Derry. The town's population increased by a staggering 51% from 2002 to 2006, with numerous large residential developments constructed on

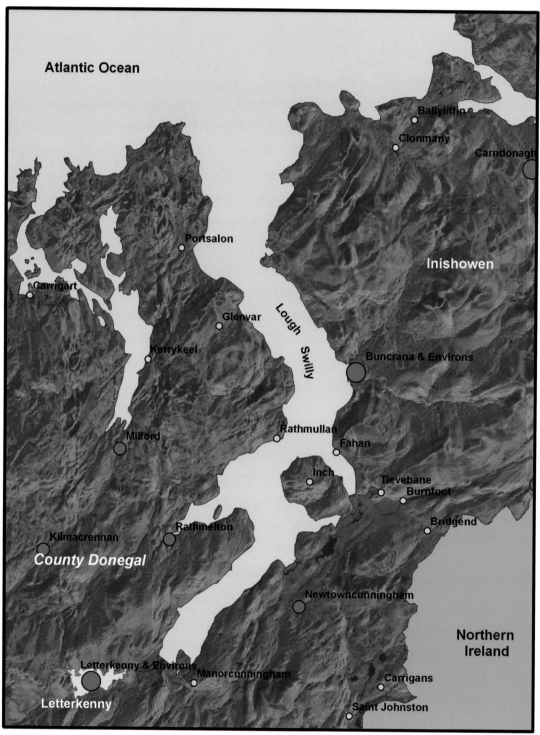

Atlantic Ocean

Ballyliffin

Clonmany

Carndonagh

Portsalon

Inishowen

Carrigart

Glenvar

Lough Swilly

Kerrykeel

Buncrana & Environs

Milford

Rathmullan

Fahan

Inch

Tievebane

Burnfoot

Bridgend

Kilmacrennan

County Donegal

Rathmelton

Newtowncunningham

**Northern
Ireland**

Letterkenny & Environs

Manorcunningham

Carrigans

Letterkenny

Saint Johnston

Towns by population

○ 0–500

● 501–1100

● 1101–18000

6.2 Distribution and size of settlements around Lough Swilly based on population numbers.

6.3 Rathmullan is located on the shores of the lough. Photo: Nigel McDowell.

6.4 Rathmullan, like other towns, is a living and evolving landscape combining old and new human activities. Photo: Nigel McDowell.

6.5 Ramelton apartments on the riverside. Photo: Nigel McDowell.

6.6 One of several of the old buildings of Ramelton that give the town its distinctive character. Photo: Nigel McDowell.

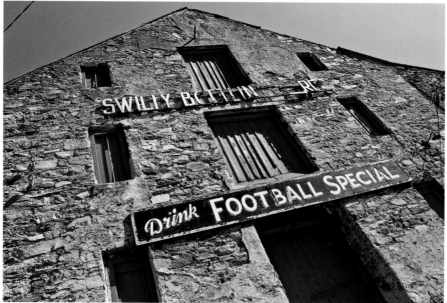

the town's peripheries. Lough Swilly is accessible at less than 3km from Newtown-cunningham and the town enjoys a prime vantage point over the lough across the Blanket Nook wildlife sanctuary.

The border town of Bridgend, along the N13 national primary route from Letterkenny to Derry, is located close to the shores of Lough Swilly. The good access routes and the supply of quality residential developments have attracted many new residents over the last number of years. Along the R238 road between Bridegend and Buncrana, and in close proximity to the shores of Lough Swilly, is the small town of Tooban, whose population has declined by 12% since 2002. With a population of just 70 people, Inch Island is one of the smaller settlements in the catchment area. Situated on the south-western corner of Inishowen, Inch Island is joined to the mainland by a causeway. The picturesque village of Fahan is situated on the Inishowen side of Lough Swilly, just 5km south of Buncrana. The Lough Swilly marina, located in the sheltered waters of Fahan, can accommodate up to 200 boats.

Located on the eastern shores of the lough, Buncrana is the second-largest town in both the catchment area and County Donegal. Buncrana is on the R238 regional road, connected to both Derry (21km distance) and Letterkenny (43km distance) via the N13 national primary road. The town has a thriving retail sector and, with many restaurants, bars, hotels and cultural activities in close proximity, is a popular tourist resort and an ideal base for exploring the Inishowen Peninsula. Buncrana boasts spectacular and panoramic views of Lough Swilly. Its natural environment plays host to many activities including golf, walking, angling and horse riding.

URBAN AND RURAL COMMUNITIES OF THE LOUGH

The people of the Lough Swilly catchment area live in either rural or urban areas, which poses the question as how to define urban and rural types. The approach

Table 6.1: Population of census towns						
Townname	Electoral area	Urban type	Pop. in 02	Pop. in 06	Size	% chg
Manorcunningham	Inishowen	S	320	414	<1,500	29.4
Kerrykeel	Letterkenny	S	253	331	<1,500	30.8
Bridgend	Inishowen	S	298	334	<1,500	12.1
Fahan	Inishowen	S	338	417	<1,500	23.4
Tooban	Inishowen	S	267	235	<1,500	-12.0
Newtowncunningham	Inishowen	M	663	999	<1,500	50.7
Ramelton	Letterkenny	M	1,051	1,088	<1,500	3.5
Rathmullan	Letterkenny	M	514	469	<1,500	-8.8
Buncrana	Inishowen	L	5,271	5,911	>5,000	12.1
Letterkenny	Letterkenny	L	15,231	17,586	>5,000	15.5

Source: CSO, 2006

6.7 One of several of the old buildings of Ramelton give that give the town its distinctive character. Photo: Nigel McDowell.

used to determine these settlement patterns utilizes data taken from the Census 2006 and the County Development Plan 2006–12.

There are ten defined census towns in the catchment area ranging in population from 331 to 17,586. The towns can be classified as small (population 150 to 500), medium (500 to 1,500) and large (1,500 to 5,000+). As Table 6.1 (above) reveals, the majority of towns are considered as small. With the exception of Rathmullan and Tooban, all of the towns experienced positive population growth from 2002 to 2006 and, in particular, Newtowncunningham experienced substantial growth of 50.7%.

In addition, there are three settlements (Glenvar, Portsalon and Inch Island) within the catchment areas that are not defined, according to the Census 2006, as census towns. However, these areas fall within the control points[5] of the County Development Plan 2006–12, and within the context of this chapter will therefore be defined as urban areas.

Table 6.2 shows the total population of these control point areas and is based on a count of the residential units[6] by the average household size of approximately 2.69 persons per household. The areas outside both the census towns and control points for the purposes of this chapter are classified as 'rural'. It is estimated, therefore, that of the 36,924 people residing in the catchment area, 28,218 (or 76%) are in the urban areas, while 8,706 persons, or 24% of the population, live in rural areas.

The impact of Letterkenny and Buncrana being the largest population centres in County Donegal is strongly reflected in the proportion in the urban category.

5 See Donegal County Development Plan 2006–12.   6 As taken from the geo-directory.

6.8 One of several of the old buildings of Ramelton. Photo: Nigel McDowell.

6.9 Letterkenny is a fast-growing urban settlement that has spread along the shores of Lough Swilly in recent years. Photo: Marianne O'Connor.

Table 6.2: Population in the Lough Swilly control points area

Towns	Electoral area	Urban type	Size	Pop. estimate in 2006
Glenvar	Letterkenny	S	<1,500	30
Portsalon	Letterkenny	S	<1,500	334
Inch Island	Inishowen	S	<1,500	70

Source: Community & Planning, Donegal County Council, Dec. 2010

6.10 The scattered rural
settlement of Fanad is
typical of much of
Lough Swilly. Photo:
Nigel McDowell.

6.11 Scattered rural
development on
Inishowen combines with
windmills to provide a
clear human imprint on
the visible landscape.
Photo: Nigel McDowell.

Travelling To and Around the Lough

Situated in the north-east of Donegal, within a county that is considered peripheral by all standards, access to the area is critical for the communities who reside around the lough and for the local economy.

ROAD NETWORK

The Lough Swilly catchment area is serviced by numerous national roads, converging in Letterkenny. Those roads include the N13 national primary road

from Letterkenny to Derry and to Ballybofey/Stranorlar, the N14 national primary road to Lifford and the N56 national secondary road. There are numerous regional and local roads, which allow for access to the more remote parts of the area.

Table 6.3 below illustrates that there is a total road length of 844km in the Lough Swilly catchment area, with 'local roads' accounting for the highest proportion there. Comparatively, the national routes account for less than 5% of the total road network.

6.12 The agricultural imprint on the landscape is dominant around much of the Swilly shoreline. Photo: Nigel McDowell.

Table 6.3: Km distance of road network		
Road type	Total km distance	% total
National primary	36.33	4.3%
National secondary	3.6	0.4%
Regional roads	78.82	9.3%
Local roads	725.74	86%
Total	**844.49**	

Source: Donegal County Council, 2010

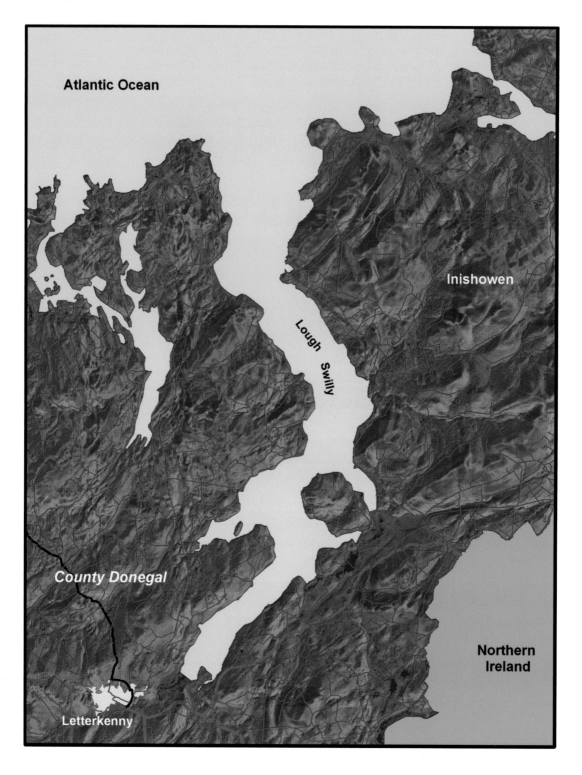

6.13 The Lough Swilly road network showing main (blue and black) and secondary (red) roads.

BUS ROUTES

The various parts of the Lough Swilly catchment area are linked together through the services of two bus operators – namely, the Lough Swilly Bus Company and North West Busways. The Lough Swilly Bus Company travels to the Fanad Peninsula through Rathmullan, Ramelton and Letterkenny on the western side of the lough and also serves the towns of Manorcunningham, Newtowncunningham, Bridgend, Fahan and Buncrana on the eastern side. There are onward connections to Derry and to west Donegal through Letterkenny.

North West Busways operate from Inishowen to Letterkenny with Buncrana, Fahan, Bridgend and Newtowncunningham benefiting from their services.

THE LOUGH SWILLY FERRY

The Lough Swilly Ferry Service commenced its first seasonal operation in late May 2004 between Buncrana and Rathmullan and due to its success it has operated subsequently every year since (2004–9). The crossing takes roughly thirty minutes and it was acknowledged from the outset that the service would be of a seasonal nature. The ferry allows visitors to cross this scenic body of water, and is an alternative to the 64km road trip.

ACCESS TO AIRPORTS AND SEA PORTS

Despite the perceived peripheral location of County Donegal it is paradoxically positioned in the centre of a 'hub of connectivity', with surprisingly low travel times to various national and international destinations. Table 6.4 below displays travel times from Letterkenny to various centres. It is important to note that an extra hour in travel time is necessary from either the Fanad or north Inishowen peninsulas to Letterkenny.

Table 6.4: Travel times to Letterkenny	
From	*Travel time to Letterkenny*
Donegal Airport	50 mins
Derry City Airport	44 mins
London Stanstead Airport	1 hour 48 mins
Sligo Airport	1 hour 58 mins
Belfast International Airport	2 hours 5 mins
Belfast Port	2 hours 8 mins
Belfast City Airport	2 hours 14 mins
Larne Port	2 hours 24 mins
Knock Airport	2 hours 32 mins
London Heathrow Airport	2 hours 55 mins
Dublin Airport	3 hours 14 mins
Galway	3 hours 46 mins
New York	8 hours 45 mins
Boston	9 hours 29 mins
Source: Research and Policy, 2009	

TRAVEL TO WORK PATTERNS IN AND AROUND LOUGH SWILLY

The above section highlights the accessibility of Lough Swilly in the wider context of County Donegal and the north-west region. This is important not only from a tourism perspective but also in terms of travelling to work and accessing services such as schools, as well as retail, cultural, community and sporting facilities etc. This section examines commuting to work patterns by the people who live around the lough.

The Western Development Commission recently carried out an analysis of the Place of Work Census of Anonymised Records (POWCAR)[7]. This report highlights twelve distinctive labour catchments[8] within County Donegal of which four are located in and around Lough Swilly.

- 'The Letterkenny catchment area' is the largest labour catchment area in the County with 17,886 people living in the area who are in work. The majority of these people work in Letterkenny – 8,562 (47.9%); Donegal Rural County[9] – 6,197 (34.6%); County Derry – 458 (2.6%); and Ballybofey/Stranorlar – 441 (2.4%). This report also highlights that in excess of 777 people (4.3% of workers) living in the Letterkenny labour catchment area travel to work in other parts of Northern Ireland; for example, 294 travel to County Tyrone, 18 to County Antrim and 7 to County Fermanagh.

- 'The Derry catchment area' is the second-largest labour catchment area in County Donegal, with a total resident working population of 4,581 people. The majority of these people work in rural Donegal – 1,761 (38.4%); County Derry – 1,490 (32.5%); Moville – 329 (7%); and Buncrana – 299 (6.5%). The report also indicates that at least 1,582 people in this area (34.5%) travel to work in Northern Ireland.

- The 'Buncrana catchment area' is the fifth-largest labour catchment area in the county with a total of 2,995 workers resident of whom 9.3% (278) travel to work in County Derry thus making it the third-most popular work destination after Buncrana and the rural parts of County Donegal. At least 299 people, or 9.5% of the resident working population, commute to work in Northern Ireland.

- The 'Carndonagh catchment area' is the eighth-largest labour catchment area within the county, with a total resident working population of 1,737. Of those workers living in the Carndonagh labour catchment 9.8% (171 persons) travel to work in County Derry, which makes it the third-most popular workplace destination for workers resident after the rural parts of County Donegal and the town of Carndonagh.

7 In 2007, the CSO compiled and made available a dataset from the 2006 Census of Population, which is referred to as the Place of Work Census of Anonymised Records (POWCAR). This dataset contains a complete count of all residents over the age of 15 years who travelled to work in April 2006, along with details of their place of residence and place of work at ED level. Western Development Commission, 2009, *Travel to Work and Labour Catchments in the Western Region: A Profile of Seven Town Labour Catchments; Western Development Commission, 2010, The County Derry Labour Catchment within County Donegal Analysis of Census of Population 2006, POWCAR data.*   8 The town labour catchments show the geographical area from which a town draws most of its labour supply.   9 Population of less than 1,000 people.

6.14 (*facing page*) The road over Mamore Gap on Inishowen is typical of the more rural parts of the Swilly catchment. Photo: Nigel McDowell.

6.15 Motorcyclists emerge from the Lough Swilly Ferry at Rathmullan. Photo: Nigel McDowell.

The above emphasizes the labour flow patterns from around the lough to different counties in Northern Ireland with 2,829 people making the journey on a daily basis.

Characteristics of the People (Demographics)

This section considers the demographics of the inhabitants; for instance, how many people fall into the different life cycles? What is the age of housing in the area? What are the predominant occupations and social classes in the area? What are the levels of educational attainment? To answer these questions raw data was extracted for each of the 22 electoral divisions falling in and around the lough in an effort to compile a single indicator for the catchment area across a number of key themes outlined below. These were then compared with the county and State averages.

LIFE CYCLES OF THE PEOPLE

Determining the life cycle of the population is an important factor in determining the services and facilities needed to cater for the needs of residents, now and into the future. As outlined above the total population of the Lough Swilly catchment areas was 36,924 persons according to the Census 2006; this figure can be divided into a number of distinctive age segments or life cycles:

- there were 3,006 children of 'preschool age' or 8% of the population;

- there were 8,437 young people of 'school going age', that is, primary, secondary and third level age, representing 23% of the population;

- 5,910 people (16%) fell into the 'early working age' stage of 20–9 years of age. This is higher than the average for the county (13%);

- there were 15,809 people (43%) at the 'working life age' of 30–65 years;

- The Lough Swilly catchment area had a lower percentage of persons falling into the 'older age' category at 10% (3,762) than that of the entire county (13%) and the State (11%).

Table 6.5: Population by life cycle and age category in the Lough Swilly catchment area, County Donegal and the State, 2006

Life cycle	Age category	Catchment area	Donegal	State
Preschool	0–4 years	8%	8%	7%
School going	5–19 years	23%	22%	20%
Early working life	20–29 years	16%	13%	17%
Working life	30–65 years	43%	44%	45%
Older adult	65+ years	10%	13%	11%

Source: Census 2006

THE FAMILY CYCLE OF PEOPLE IN THE LOUGH

At any stage a family can be at a different cycle with regards to children. Tables 6.6(a) and 6.6(b) below highlight the number of couples with no children, and the number of couples with children, by their family cycle in the catchment area, County Donegal and the State. Table 6.6(a) illustrates that 41% (931) of couples are at the 'pre-family cycle' in the Lough Swilly catchment area compared to 31% of couples (or 3,031) in County Donegal. In addition, 38% of couples with no children are at the 'empty nest' part of the cycle and 21% at the 'retired cycle' in the Lough Swilly catchment area, both of which are lower than the equivalent rates for the county and the State.[10]

Table 6.6(a): Total number of couples with no children by family cycle in the Lough Swilly catchment area, County Donegal and the State, 2006

	Pre-family	Empty nest	Retired	Total couples
State	129,828	109,955	63771	303,554
%	**43%**	**36%**	**21%**	
Donegal County	3,013	4,230	2,373	9,616
%	**31%**	**44%**	**25%**	
Catchment area	931	878	482	2,291
%	**41%**	**38%**	**21%**	

Source: Census 2006

10 'pre-family cycle': family nucleus of husband and wife or cohabiting couple where the wife is under 45 years; 'empty nest': family nucleus of husband and wife or cohabiting couple where the wife is aged 45–64 years; 'retired cycle': family nucleus of husband and wife or cohabiting couple where the wife is aged 65 years and over.

Table 6.6(b): Total number of family units with children by family cycle[11] in the Lough Swilly catchment area, County Donegal and the State, 2006

	Pre-school	Early school	Pre-adolescent	Adolescent	Adult	Total
State	118,832	116,776	110,109	131,371	272,538	749,626
%	**16%**	**16%**	**15%**	**18%**	**36%**	
Donegal County	4,113	4,248	4,230	5,024	9,710	27,325
%	**15%**	**16%**	**15%**	**18%**	**36%**	
Catchment area	1,125	1,151	1,098	1,213	2,097	6,684
%	**17%**	**17%**	**16%**	**18%**	**31%**	

Source: Census 2006

The catchment area of Lough Swilly had a higher percentage of family units where the oldest child was at 'preschool' age (17%). In addition 17% were at the 'early-school' age and 16% at the 'pre-adolescence' stage, all of which are higher than for County Donegal or the State as a whole.[12] The youthful age structure of the Lough Swilly catchment area is emphasized with a lower percentage of family units where the oldest child is aged as 'adult' at 20 years and over.

HOUSING

There were 29,290 persons living in permanent private households in the catchment area at the time of the Census 2006. It would appear that the upturn experienced in the economy from 1998 to the compilation of the statistics contained in Table 6.7 had an impact on the housing sector in the Swilly catchment. A slightly higher percentage of the population (22%) was residing in households constructed post-2001 in and around Lough Swilly than for that of County Donegal (20%) or the State (17%). Correspondingly, there is a marginally lower percentage of the population residing in older type households, that is, built pre-1970, in and around Lough Swilly than for the County (22% compared to 24%) and a substantially lower percentage than in the State (31%).

WORKING LIFE

The Lough Swilly catchment area has 16,931 persons who are in the labour force,[13] giving the catchment area a higher labour force participation rate[14] (60%) than the County (57%), but lower than the State (62%). Of these, 14,729 persons are at work. This is 26% of the total number of persons at work in County Donegal

11 Couples or lone parents with children by family cycle.   12 'preschool': 0–4 years; 'early-school': 5–9 years; 'pre-adolescence': 10–14 years.   13 The total labour force is calculated as the sum of the unemployed plus first-time job seekers plus total number of persons at work.   14 This is calculated as the total labour force divided by the total persons aged 15 years and over.

Table 6.7: Number of persons in permanent private households by year house
built in the Lough Swilly catchment area, County Donegal and the State, 2006

Year	Catchment area		Donegal County		State	
Pre 1919	2,208	8%	12,902	9%	364,339	9%
1919–40	1,034	4%	6,505	5%	259,682	6%
1941–60	1,587	5%	7,714	5%	362,419	9%
1961–70	1,354	5%	7,516	5%	300,512	7%
1971–80	3,860	13%	20,684	14%	635,037	15%
1981–90	4,693	16%	23,812	17%	533,621	13%
1991–95	2,915	10%	12,653	9%	296,565	7%
1996–2000	4,358	15%	20,351	14%	486,686	12%
2001 or later	6504	22%	28,304	20%	682,479	17%
Not stated	777	3%	2,924	2%	185,413	5%
Total persons	**29,290**		**143,365**		**4,106,753**	

Source: Census 2006

Table 6.8: Persons aged 15 years and over by principal economic status in the
Lough Swilly catchment area, County Donegal and the State, 2006

	Catchment area	County Donegal	State
Total in labour force	16,931	65,092	2,109,498
Total not in labour force	11,343	48,746	1,265,901
Unemployment rate	13%	13%	9%
Labour force participation rate	60%	57%	62%
Non-participation rate	40%	43%	38%
Total aged 15 years and over	**28,274**	**113,838**	**3,375,399**

Source: Census 2006

(56,670). Of the persons at work in this catchment area 8,226 were male and 6,503
were female.

According to the Census 2006, males in the catchment area were mainly
employed as 'building and construction workers' (17.7%), 'manufacturing workers'
(16.3%) and 'professional workers' (15.5%). Females in the catchment area were
most likely to be employed as 'professional workers' (28.5%), 'service workers'
(20.7%) and as 'clerical workers' (16.8%).

SOCIAL CLASS OF THE LABOUR FORCE

One of the general trends in County Donegal over the last number of years has
been an increase in the percentage of the population falling into the higher social
class or professional classes (Social Classes 1 & 2) and a decrease in the numbers
falling into the lower skilled social classes (Social Class 6 & 7).

Table 6.9: Social class of the population in the Lough Swilly catchment area,
County Donegal and the State, 2006

	Population 2006	Pop. social class 1 (%)	Pop. social class 2 (%)	Pop. social class 3 (%)	Pop. social class 4 (%)	Pop. social class 5 (%)	Pop. social class 6 (%)	Pop. social class 7 (%)
Catchment area	36,924	5.8%	25.6%	16.7%	17.4%	11.4%	5.2%	17.9%
County Donegal	147,264	4.0%	23.6%	16.3%	20.0%	13.7%	5.9%	16.6%
State	4,239,848	6.5%	26.4%	17.0%	17.1%	11.1%	4.3%	17.6%

Source: Gamma, 2006

Table 6.10: Population in school, university and other education in the Lough
Swilly catchment area, County Donegal and the State, 2006

	Total	Males	Females
Catchment area	4,489	2,061	2,428
Donegal County	15,165	6,930	8,235
State	525,066	252,163	272,903

Source: Census 2006

In 2006, the percentage of the population falling into the higher social classes in the catchment area of Lough Swilly was 31.4% (or 11,583), which was on par with the State average of 32.9%, but 4% above the average for County Donegal (27.5%). The percentage of the population falling into the lower skilled social classes was marginally higher in the Swilly catchment area at 23.1% (or 8,543) than that for either County Donegal (22.5%) or the State (21.9%).

EDUCATIONAL ATTAINMENT LEVELS

The education of a child or young person can shape their own personal development and life chances, as well as the economic and social progress of the area; therefore, it is interesting to examine educational attainment levels around the lough. In the catchment area of Lough Swilly 12.2% (or 4,489 persons) were still in full-time education or at school, college or other training. This compares with 10.3% of the population for County Donegal and 12.4% for the State as a whole.

In 2006, 23,068 persons had completed their full-time education in the catchment area of which:

- 5,689 persons had no formal or primary education,
- 5,138 had a lower secondary education,
- 4,000 had an upper secondary education,
- 1,577 had a technical or vocational education,
- 6,664 had a third-level education.

From the analysis it is evident that the people of Lough Swilly attained higher educational standards than in County Donegal as a whole. In the catchment area a higher percentage of the population had a third-level qualification (29%) than in the county as a whole (23%). Lough Swilly had a higher percentage of the population who had finished their education with 'no formal or primary education' (25%) than in the State (19%), but a lower percentage than in the county (30%).

Lifestyles

A number of important factors impact on the quality of a person's lifestyle, including the availability of childcare, play areas, primary and secondary schools, and networking opportunities etc. To determine where children go to school, where children play, where people can network and where people can engage in the arts, a 10km-distance band was placed from the central point of each of the twenty-two Electoral Divisions in the catchment area and the number of services within that distance to be accurately calculated using a computerized Geographic Information System (GIS). The distance band of 10km extends well beyond the Lough Swilly catchment area, but is generally accepted as the maximum distance that people will travel to avail of particular services.

CHILDCARE

There are 3,006 children of pre-school age, ranging from 0–4 years of age, in the defined catchment area. This represents 8.1% of the entire population of the area.

Table 6.11: Education attainment levels in the Lough Swilly catchment area, County Donegal and the State, 2006

	Pop. no formal or primary education only (%)	Pop. lower secondary education (%)	Pop. upper secondary education (%)	Pop. technical vocational education (%)	Pop. third-level education (%)
Catchment area	25%	22%	17%	7%	29%
County Donegal	30%	24%	17%	7%	23%
State	19%	21%	21%	9%	30%

Source: Census 2006

There are 10 types of services offered for children ranging from 0 to 6 years, including full day care, pre-school, sessional, and parent and toddler groups. There are a total of 81 childcare facilities available within 10km – which represents approximately 47% of the total provided in the county. Letterkenny and Buncrana, with larger numbers of pre-school children requiring services, have a strong impact on those numbers in the catchment area.

PLAY FACILITIES

For the youth population of the area, particularly from ages 0 to 12 years, there are 16 playgrounds available within 10km. These are located in Rossnakill, Rathmullan (2), Milford, Ramelton, Letterkenny (5), Manorcunningham, Newtowncunningham (2), Buncrana (2) and Ballyliffin. In addition, there are mini-pitches in Letterkenny and Newtowncunningham, available to all age groups.

SCHOOL INFRASTRUCTURE

In the catchment area a combined total of 8,437 students (5 to 19 years of age) attend primary and secondary schools. There are 62 primary schools within 10km, and 10 secondary schools. The latter are located in Milford (2), Letterkenny (4), Raphoe (2) and Buncrana (2).

There are 4,489 people in full-time education in college or in a training facility. The Letterkenny Institute of Technology (LYIT) provides third-level education within the area. The college offers 25 study areas across 11 departments and has an enrolment of 2,562 full-time and 483 part-time students.[15] In addition, FÁS, the national training agency, has a training centre in Letterkenny offering a wide range of courses.

COMMUNITY INFRASTRUCTURE

There is a vibrant community and voluntary sector in the lough's hinterland. People can access 221 community and voluntary groups[16] within 10km, with notable concentrations in north Fanad and Rossnakill, Letterkenny, Newtown-cunningham, Buncrana and Clonmany. This area contains 38% of the county's known community groups serving an eclectic mix of interest-groups concerned with tourism, housing and residential issues, festivals, older people, sports and recreation, and literary affairs.

CULTURAL INFRASTRUCTURE

Culture can make an immense contribution to people's quality of life. The study area offers a vast array of cultural activities across many sectors including heritage, language, music, drama and visual arts. In total 29% (124) of the county's cultural infrastructure (cultural practitioners, providers and faculties) is located in the

---

15 As in October 2008.   16 Research and Policy, 2006, *The Donegal Community Audit: A Strategic Needs Assessment.*

6.16 Public art at
Rathmullan: the Flight
of the Earls statue.
Photo: Nigel McDowell.

catchment area and accessible within a 10km distance. There are clusters of cultural activities in Rathmullan, Ramelton, Buncrana and Clonmany. Letterkenny again accounts for a significant proportion of cultural infrastructure and includes An Grianan Theatre, the Regional Cultural Centre, the County Museum and the Central Library.

Also, there are five branch libraries in Milford, Ramelton, Raphoe, Buncrana and Clonmany. Taobh Tíre is an initiative of Donegal County Council that seeks to improve library services to rural and isolated communities across County Donegal. At a 10km distance, Swilly residents can access five Taobh Tíre Service Points in Fanavolty, Fanad, Letterkenny (2) and St Johnston.

Table 6.12: Private households headed by a lone parent in the Lough Swilly catchment area, County Donegal and the State, 2006

	Total private hhlds	Lone father with children	Lone mother with children	Lone father with children and other persons	Lone mother with children and other persons	Total headed by a lone parent
State	1,469,521	21,689	130,853	3,244	13,994	169,780
% of Private Hhlds		**1.5%**	**8.9%**	**0.2%**	**1.0%**	**11.6%**
Donegal County	50,415	809	4,949	66	409	6,233
% of Private Hhlds		**1.6%**	**9.8%**	**0.1%**	**0.8%**	**12.3%**
Catchment area	12,608	170	1,385	18	111	1,684
% of Private Hhlds		**1.3%**	**11.0%**	**0.1%**	**0.9%**	**13.3%**

Source: Census 2006

Table 6.13: Percentage of persons outside the labour force by main reason for non-participation in the Lough Swilly catchment area, County Donegal and the State, 2006

	Catchment area	County Donegal	State
Student	29%	23%	28%
Looking after home/family	29%	32%	31%
Retired	28%	31%	30%
Unable to work due to permanent sickness or disability	13%	14%	11%
Other	1%	1%	1%

Source: Census 2006

The Challenges Faced by Lough Swilly's Residents

To plan for an inclusive society requires an in-depth understanding of the factors or characteristics of the population that can result in people being excluded. This section examines some of these characteristics.

LONE PARENTS

There are 12,608 private households located in the Lough Swilly catchment area, of which 13.3% (or 1,684) are headed by a lone parent. This is higher than in County Donegal or in the State, at 12.3% and 11.6% respectively.

PERSONS NOT PARTICIPATING IN THE LABOUR FORCE

In the study area, 40% of all persons 15 years and over (or 11,343 persons) do not participate in the labour force; this figure is lower than the county average of 43%, but higher than the State average of 38%. The main reason cited by people for non-labour force participation in the Lough Swilly area is to 'look after the home/

family' (3,345 people), closely followed by the reasons of being a 'student' (3,264 people) or being 'retired' (3,212 people).

PEOPLE WHO ARE UNEMPLOYED

Although 16,931 persons in the Lough Swilly catchment area are participating in the labour force, 13%[17] (or 2,202 persons) are unemployed or first-time job seekers. This figure is marginally higher than the unemployment rate for the county (12.9%) and substantially higher than the rate for the State (8.5%).

PEOPLE WITH A DISABILITY

There are a total of 3,626 persons in the Lough Swilly catchment area who have some form of disability. In common with the county and State trends, the majority of people with a disability in and around the lough fall into the older age category of '65 years and over' (35%) and the '45–64 years' (27%). The catchment area also has a higher percentage of its population with a disability falling into the younger age categories of '0–14 years', '15–24 years' and '25–44 years' than in County Donegal.

PEOPLE LIVING ALONE OVER 65 YEARS

As noted above, there are 3,762 persons falling into the older age category (65 years and over) in the catchment area of Lough Swilly, of which 24% or 904 persons are living alone. As a percentage of total private households this is lower than the average for the County (10%) or for the State (8%).

Table 6.14: Total number of people with a disability in the Lough Swilly catchment area, County Donegal and the State, 2006

Age group	0–14	15–24	25–44	45–64	65 and over	Total
Catchment area	372	308	693	994	1,259	3,626
%	10%	8%	19%	27%	35%	
Donegal County	1,282	1,035	2589	4,358	5,717	14,981
%	9%	7%	17%	29%	38%	
State	33,256	29,047	78,326	114,899	138,257	393,785
%	8%	7%	20%	29%	35%	

Source: Census 2006

Table 6.15: Persons with a disability by age group in the Lough Swilly catchment area, County Donegal and the State, 2006

	Total private households 2006	Persons living alone 45+	Persons living alone 65+	Persons living alone 45+ (%)	Persons living alone 65+(%)
Catchment area	12,608	1,758	904	14%	7%
Donegal	50,415	8,756	5,058	17%	10%
National	1,469,521	223,115	121,157	15%	8%

Source: Census 2006

17 This is calculated as (unemployed + first-time job seekers)/ total labour force.

Table 6.16: Number of permanent private households by type of occupancy in the Lough Swilly catchment area, County Donegal and the State, 2006

Occupancy	Owner occupied with mortgage	Owner occupied no mortgage	Buying from Local Authority	Rented from Local Authority	Rented from Voluntary Body	Other rented – unfurnished	Other rented – furnished	Occupied free of rent	Not stated
Catchment area	4,447	4,394	176	1,017	654	173	1,200	201	295
%	35%	35%	1%	8%	5%	1%	10%	2%	2%
Donegal County	16,364	22,303	812	3,604	1,635	557	2,670	1,005	1,043
%	33%	45%	2%	7%	3%	1%	5%	2%	2%
State	569,966	498,432	23,547	105,509	50,480	16,621	128,696	21,701	47,344
%	39%	34%	2%	7%	3%	1%	9%	1%	3%

Source: Census 2006

HOUSEHOLD TYPE BY OCCUPANCY

In 2006 there were 12,557 permanent private households in the catchment area around Lough Swilly. The rented proportion of these in the catchment area of Lough Swilly accounted for 26% (or 3,248 households) compared to 18% being rented in County Donegal and 21% in the State. In addition, the Lough Swilly catchment area had a lower percentage of its permanent private households that are owner-occupied without a mortgage than in the county as a whole – 35% versus 45%.

STRATEGIC PLANNING

The vast majority of the people living in and around Lough Swilly are categorized as an urban population. While in many respects the characteristics of the population of the lough mirrors that of the county and the State as a whole, it differs in some ways; it has a more modern housing stock and it appears that its inhabitants are younger families and better educated. Despite a high proportion of the labour force finding work in the labour catchment area around the lough, there is a flow of workers commuting across the border on a daily basis. Anecdotal evidence suggests that there is also substantial activity on a cross-border basis to avail of other types of services and functions including retail, health services, tourism etc.

The overall aim of the spatial strategy as contained in the County Development Plan, 2006–12 is to 'create a more prosperous county with an improved quality of life by providing the focus and support necessary to create strong urban structures and sustainable areas'. The implementation of this strategy will impact on all of the inhabitants who live around Lough Swilly. The key aims of the Plan are:

- to create a vibrant and fully functioning Letterkenny–Derry linked gateway as the principal driver for the development of the region.

- to create through urban strengthening measures strong urban structures at sub-gateway level, which according to this plan, have the capacity to consolidate the gateway and ensure that a network exists to filter and funnel the benefits of the gateway to all parts of the county. The towns in and around the lough that fall into this category are Buncrana, Bridgend, Newtowncunningham and Ramelton.

- to manage the growth in close proximity to the gateways through urban support measures. This will impact on the towns of Fahan and Manorcunningham.

- to create vibrant rural areas, the key drivers of a changing rural economy, by providing support for rural villages and rural communities.

- to safeguard the role of centres with special functions that will impact on a number of towns including Rathmullan.

It is clear that Letterkenny, as an important 'growth centre' strongly influence the demographic character of the Swilly population discussed here. Many fewer people live in the large surrounding areas that are mainly rural in character. It is the authors' hope that the various spacial strategies being implemented by Donegal County Council will act to spread prosperity from this core to the more peripheral regions of the Swilly catchment in the years ahead.

Chapter 7

Nature Conservation

Andrew Speer

Introduction

Lough Swilly, being one of the most significant coastal features in the north-west of Ireland, is not only a major resource for humans but also for the wildlife that use it. Its geographical position in a global context is important. It sits on the westernmost corner of the European–Asian landmass and on the eastern edge of the Atlantic Ocean, a fact that undoubtedly enhances its conservation interest and biodiversity.

Lough Swilly could be likened to a motorway service station for wildlife migrating along the fringes of Europe. From that perspective it has been particularly recognized as an important area for birds and mammals. Its deep entrance and shallow margins make it an ideal home for the many marine species that utilize it.

The natural heritage value of Lough Swilly is linked to both the land and the sea. It is easy to visualize the marine aspect of the lough and also the terrestrial aspect of the lough and adjoining land, but the inter-tidal area in between the two is also very significant. Often it is that area that requires most effort regarding conservation. Lough Swilly hosts a wide diversity of species from large marine mammals to small birds and even microscopic plankton. As in other areas, the value of the natural resources of a given area was directly related to it providing food and resources of value to humans. Lough Swilly is no exception and the communities of people living around it have, over the years, depended on the lough for their needs.

Nature conservation seeks to preserve living habitats in the face of threats from various quarters. The challenge for the conservation of the lough and its ecology is finding a balance between protecting the ecosystem while allowing people to use it 'sustainably' to meet their own needs. This process of constantly finding and maintaining the balance is a challenge that requires establishing a certain level of protection and then monitoring the situation. Having a good understanding of the natural habitats and of existing and planned human activities is essential. The Department of Environment, Heritage and Local Government is the government department with responsibility for the designation and protection of wildlife habitats, species and areas of conservation interest throughout Ireland. The National Parks and Wildlife Service (NPWS) is the organization within that department with direct responsibility for the conservation of biodiversity and wildlife under the Wildlife Acts (1976 and 2000), the EU Habitat Regulations (1997) and the EU Bird Regulations (1997).

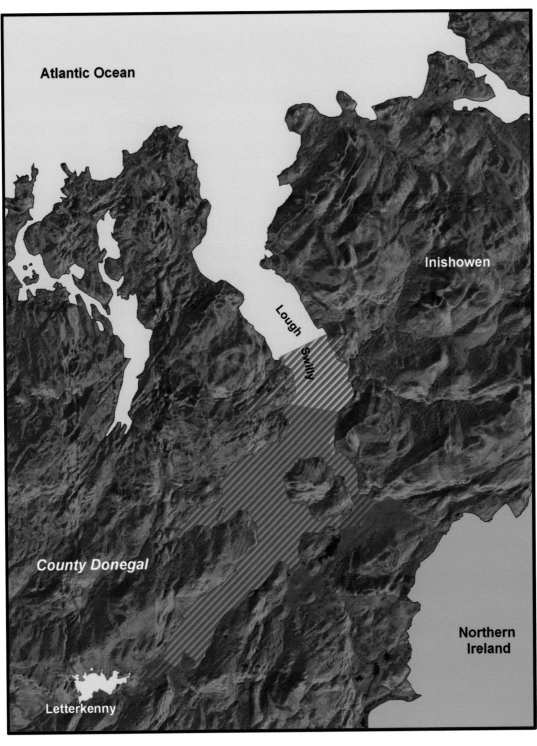

SPA Areas 2011
SAC Areas 2011

7.1 Map of conservation designations in and around Lough Swilly.

7.2 Aerial view of Inch Wildfowl Reserve. Photo: Emmett Johnston.

Conservation initiatives in the lough are currently being undertaken at various levels, from national government to local volunteers. Government implements conservation legislation in Lough Swilly, the most direct outcome of which is the designation of sites for their conservation value. Monitoring of the lough is undertaken by government and NGOs (Non-Government Organizations), such as Birdwatch Ireland, who have been recording bird numbers on Lough Swilly for over twenty years, and the IWDG (Irish Whale and Dolphin Group), who have been recording cetaceans in the waters of Lough Swilly. Pressure groups such as Save the Swilly, Coastwatch and Buncrana Environmental Group to name a few, have been active around the lough, highlighting issues; this too helps the efforts of conservation authorities striving to maintain a balance.

Lough Swilly has a variety of habitats below and above the tide. Many are simply remnants of habitats such as ancient woodlands and salt marshes, that at one time would have been much more extensive. These give a glimpse of what the lough would have looked like in the past. Humans have altered Lough Swilly in recent times with embankments to prevent tidal flooding along long stretches of the shoreline and the transformation of salt marshes and tidal flats to farmland and lakes. In a strange twist, the artificial farmland created by this loss of natural habitat is now considered worthy of conservation, due to its importance for wintering wildfowl.

Conservation Designations

Lough Swilly is listed as a Ramsar Site (an internationally important wetland) as well as being a Special Area of Conservation (SAC) for its habitats and a Special Protection Area (SPA) for its bird life under European legislation. It is also designated a Natural Heritage Area by Irish law. These designations give Lough Swilly status on a global stage, but more importantly offer a degree of legal protection. Without an understanding of the importance of the lough at a local level, however, legislation can only go so far in conserving it.

A considerable part of Lough Swilly is designated as a Special Area of Conservation (SAC). Ireland transposed the EU Habitats and Birds Directive into Irish law in 1997, and shortly after it presented a list of sites for SAC designation including Lough Swilly. The process of designating any site takes some time, allowing for appeals and any subsequent boundary changes, but Lough Swilly is now recognized formally as an SAC (site code 2287) and the Irish government is charged with its protection and status. The boundaries stretch from Letterkenny in the south-west to Buncrana in the north-east. Primarily the site is inter-tidal and sub-tidal, but also includes areas of native woodland along its shores and incorporates one state-owned National Nature Reserve at Rathmullan Wood. Inch Wildfowl Reserve is also included within the boundaries of the SAC, as it is classified as a Brackish Lagoon. This site is of conservation importance as it contains good examples of at least four habitats listed on Annex I of the EU Habitats Directive (estuaries, lagoons, Atlantic salt meadows, old oak woods) and supports a population of otter.

Lough Swilly also has a significant part of its inter-tidal and sub-tidal areas designated as a Special Protection Area (SPA) specifically for birds. These areas are considered for designation if they have significant national or international numbers of birds resident in winter or breeding in summer; Lough Swilly has both, with 16 species occurring regularly in numbers of national importance, plus 3 species occurring within the site and on adjacent polders in numbers of international importance. Until late 2010 the SPA boundary was confined to the main inter-tidal estuarine sections of the lough; since then the SPA boundary has increased to include more sub-tidal areas further north. The new boundary also includes an area of intensive agricultural land and has incorporated Inch Lake into one larger SPA, Lough Swilly (site code 4075).

The basic designation for wildlife in Ireland is the Natural Heritage Area (NHA) and the lough also holds this designation. This is an area considered important for the habitats present, or which holds species of plants and animals whose habitat needs protection. Its legal protection is achieved under Irish legislation (1976 Wildlife Act, amended in 2000). The shores of the lough are also home to a healthy population of otters, a species for which the site was designated as a Special Area of Conservation.

7.3 View of Inch Lake
showing the quiet
water environments.
Photo: Andrew Speer.

Some Conservation Initiatives

THE INISHOWEN BASKING SHARK SURVEY

The Inishowen Basking Shark Survey was launched in 2009 to study the basking
shark population in Inishowen coastal waters including Lough Swilly. It was
designed to refine survey methodology and survey skills; it was part funded by the
Heritage Council and was supported by the University of Ulster and the National
Parks and Wildlife Service.

The survey also aimed to promote and demonstrate responsible interaction with
the sharks to local marine users, along with raising awareness to the general public,
while, at the same time, getting a snapshot of the distribution of the basking sharks

7.4 Whooper swans at Inch Lake. Photo: Andrew Speer.

7.5 Basking shark tagged in Lough Swilly as part of a research programme to better understand their movements and assist their conservation. Photo: Nigel Motyer.

in Inishowen coastal waters. The survey involved long hours watching from boats travelling in straight lines and recording any sharks seen. The public were encouraged to report any sightings online via a dedicated website. The sharks were also tagged by the researchers and photographed for future identification.

INCH ISLET SANDWICH TERN COLONY

Sandwich terns (*Sterna sandvicensis*) are listed as an Annex 1 species on the EU Birds Directive, which means that they are considered a globally threatened species that requires particular conservation action. The sandwich terns migrate each year to spend the winter in the warmth of western Africa and return to Lough Swilly to

7.6 A tagged sandwich tern on Lough Swilly. Their numbers are being monitored in a conservation programme. Photo: Andrew Speer.

raise their young. The safe nesting habitat and easy access to the lough for a ready supply of food make this an ideal place to spend the summer.

There is a small islet in the lake at Inch Wildfowl Reserve where efforts have been made for over 20 years to enhance the habitat for breeding terns, both common and sandwich, by Dr Ken Perry who has been studying this species. High water levels (due to increased summer rainfall) became a threat to the unfledged chicks and some sort of intervention was needed. National Parks and Wildlife Service (NPWS) was able to access resources and funding to raise the levels on the island where the terns nested so as to decrease the threat of flooding and negotiate with the OPW (Office of Public Works) to prioritize maintenance of the site's sluice gates in order to reduce the threat of flooding from the sea. NPWS also appealed to Donegal Creameries (who manage the fishing on Inch Lake) to ban all boats from the lake so as to minimize disturbance to both breeding and migratory birds. As a result of these combined measures and support from the relevant stakeholders the number of sandwich terns has increased.

GREENLAND WHITE-FRONTED GOOSE STUDY

Lough Swilly has the second-largest flock of Greenland white-fronted geese in Ireland, with average numbers of 1,100 individuals. The Greenland white-fronted goose has been of conservation concern for many years. Declining numbers from the 1950s to the late 1970s prompted a debate about the effectiveness of protection measures and the Greenland white-fronted goose study was set up in 1978, together with the initiation of studies on the breeding grounds in Greenland. A network of

7.7 A tagged Greenland white-fronted goose in flight. Photo: Andrew Speer.

7.8. A Greenland white-fronted goose grazing on Inch Lake. Photo: Andrew Speer.

observers was established in 1982 to undertake regular winter counts at all the known haunts to monitor the changes in abundance of the entire population. The law was changed to protect the population from hunting in Ireland and Scotland from 1983 onwards. A programme of research was also initiated that included regular capture and marking of individuals at the Wexford Slob lands by the National Parks and Wildlife Service in Ireland. In February 2010 this programme was extended to the flock of geese in Lough Swilly, when 32 individuals were caught, marked with rings, and released. More information will now be gained through regular monitoring of the flock, showing how these individual geese interact and were they travel throughout the year and during their migration.

Nature Conservation Highlights

INCH WILDFOWL RESERVE

This site is found on the east shore of Lough Swilly, approximately 8km south of Buncrana. It supports a wide diversity of wintering waterfowl, notably swans and geese, as well as breeding terns, gulls and duck. It is an important link in the overall Lough Swilly wetland system, which includes Blanket Nook and Big Isle.

Inch Lake was created in the mid-nineteenth century when two embankments were built to link Inch Island to the mainland. A railway embankment was then built, dividing the area into an inner part (Inch Levels) that was further drained to create polders for agricultural use, while the outer part (Inch Lake) acted as a holding reservoir for drainage water. Sluice gates in the western (Farland) embankment allow drainage to the sea at low tide. Some seepage of seawater back into the lake creates brackish water conditions. Inch Lake supports a lagoonal flora, with well-developed charophyte (water plant) communities, including a large population of *Chara canescens* (a Red Data Book species).[1] It also supports horned pondweed (*Zannichellia palustris*) and a mixed pondweed/tassleweed community (*Potamogeton pectinatus/Ruppia maritima*). The aquatic fauna at Inch is rich and diverse and includes a range of lagoonal specialists and species that are apparently rare.

The lake is surrounded by wet grassland vegetation, which varies in wetness depending on water levels within the lake. The extensive polders to the east and south of the lake (Inch Levels) are included in the wildfowl reserve. These lands are farmed intensively, primarily for grass, cereals and potatoes, and provide important feeding areas for wintering waterfowl, especially geese and swans.

The National Parks and Wildlife Service manages the reserve, which is leased on a long-term agreement from Donegal Creameries, plc, which owns the adjoining Grianan Farm, one of the largest in the country. The reserve is open to the public and access is provided by paths around the lake that make use of the existing embankments. Bird hides provide good viewing and car parks are provided. Conservation work on the site is ongoing, with pro-active management providing suitable breeding, roosting and feeding habitat for a variety of species.

The combination within this site of extensive feeding areas and safe resting and roosting sites makes this site one of the most important wetlands in the north-west of the country for wintering waterfowl. Two species, whooper swan and greylag goose, occur in numbers of international importance – greylag geese numbers fluctuate depending on the weather (2008 peaked at 3,000+). Considerably higher numbers of whooper swan (peak of 6,000+) have been recorded, especially early in the season, as this is the area where the swans make their Irish landfall in autumn on their return from breeding grounds in Iceland. Three species occur in nationally important numbers (Greenland white-fronted goose, sandwich tern and common tern).

With wetter summers and higher waters levels, breeding sandwich terns are finding it increasingly difficult to raise chicks. NPWS tried to overcome this

---

1 An international list of plant and animal species at risk.

7.9 A large flock of brent geese fly over the Swilly. Photo: Andrew Speer.

problem by creating a nesting platform above the high water on a small islet in the lough. The chicks born here have had tiny rings with individual numbers put on their legs to identify each bird in later life as part of a long-term project started in 1989.

As wet grassland becomes more rare throughout the country, wading birds are finding it harder to locate suitable habitat in which to breed. NPWS are also managing the extensive wet grasslands for waders around the lake edge, by topping with tractors and mowers grazing and controlling rush and scrub, all to provide the birds with a suitable habitat to lay eggs, hide the chicks and find food. Donegal Creameries are also working with the NPWS in a farm agreement under which the geese and swans are provided with suitable feeding on the fields during the winter months.

WESTERN SHORE FROM LETTERKENNY TO RATHMULLAN WOOD

The western shore has some small remnants of old woodlands and some magnificent trees along its edge. It is beautiful place to visit with the combination of the shoreline and its birds with a backdrop of trees and streams. Oak woodlands mixed with birch, hazel and holly would have been the main woodland type here with a rich ground flora. Rathmullan Wood is a National Nature Reserve and is approximately 30ha in size. It is dominated by sessile oak (*Quercus petraea*) and

7.10 Greylag geese feeding at Inch Lake. Photo: Andrew Speer.

birch (*Betula pubescens*), but many other species are present including exotics such as beech (*Fagus sylvatica*). Alder (*Alnus glutinosa*) and willows (*Salix spp.*) occur in the wetter parts. It is open to the public with paths for easy access.

CHALLENGES FOR NATURE CONSERVATION

The natural heritage of Lough Swilly continues to face significant threats from human activity. There will always be arguments for further development on, and around, the lough, to harvest more of its marine life, to develop further aquaculture activity, to increase and develop leisure facilities. There is also the risk of pollution through discharges from land-based activities. Development has increased around the lough in recent years with single houses, urban development and leisure facilities all having knock-on effects on conservation through direct habitat loss and discharge of sewage into the lough. With increased affluence more leisure traffic is present on the lough, including small planes and boats. All human activity has potential implications for nature conservation and the ongoing challenge is to achieve a balance between such activity and conservation goals.

Chapter 8

Fishing and Shellfishing in the Twentieth and Twenty-First Centuries

John Niven

Introduction

For many coastal communities, the closest connection between people and the natural environment exists in the fishing sector. Its members, through their daily work, have a unique communion with nature. The hunter-gatherer lifestyle of the earliest fishermen continues to the present day in the Swilly fishing community. To a large extent, modern fishing practice is built on the accumulated knowledge of past generations of fishermen; for example, local fishermen know that the best months for herring fishing around Inch Island are November to February, that some of the best areas for drift netting are at Ray (south of Rathmullan) and Ball Green between the Leannan and Swilly rivers, and that if you catch herring on the ebb tide in Mill Bay, Inch Island, it's a sign that the herring are leaving. The years have shown that Lough Swilly fishermen have needed to be resourceful and adaptable. The long history of maritime trade is continued and today seafood from the lough is landed for consumption, not only in Ireland, but also in all the countries of the EU and further afield. This chapter is concerned with the recent and ongoing culture associated with fishing activity in the lough.

Lough Swilly is home to a great diversity of fish species, several of which have been fished commercially over the years. The herring fishery was historically the most important. The herring entered Lough Swilly to spawn on the seagrass (*Zostera*) beds around Inch Island, Fahan, and the estuaries of the Swilly and Leannan rivers. They were followed by cod who gorged on the herring and their spawn. A line fishery for cod was pursued after the herring fishing until the cod had their fill and moved out of the lough, following the shoals elsewhere. In the eighteenth and nineteenth century whitefish was never as important as herring in the Swilly but it filled in the quiet times and was useful for domestic consumption. The Ordnance Survey memoirs of 1834 list a wide variety of fish landed, mostly caught by lines from drontheims. At that time a cod cost *6d.*, mullet *6d.* per lb, and 10lb of flounders could be bought for *6d.* Among the other varieties available were haddock, sole, turbot, ling and skate, all of which are still to be found in some abundance.

Herring Drift Netting

Drift netting for herring was traditionally carried on by boats from all around the lough – from Castlegrove in the River Swilly to Doaghbeg near Fanad Head and from Inch Island to Leenankeel on the Dunaff side. The fishing started in June or July and employed around 200 boats. During the 1920s a different herring fishery was carried on in springtime seaward of the Swilly by Scottish steam drifters who landed their catch in Buncrana. They called it the 'May fishing'. The Swilly herring have always been small but with a distinctive flavour and so were always in demand. A local team of pair trawlers landed up to 700 tonnes of herring a season in recent years, finding a ready market in the fish processing plants of Killybegs.

Herring drift nets are vertical curtains of netting that drift with the tide. They can be set at various depths as the herring swim at different levels in the water according to weather conditions and other factors. The mesh size must be suitable for the particular herring stock being fished and the amount of net set depends on the abundance of fish in the area. If fish are scarce, set more net. If fish are plentiful, fishermen were often not able to handle all they caught. If that happened, it was (and remains to this day) common practice to give the extra nets and fish to another boat. They would return the net the next night after extracting the fish.

Trawling

Trawling is a method of fishing that involves towing a large cone-shaped net along the bottom of the sea. The net is kept open in the correct shape by 'otter boards' or trawl doors, which are rigged to shear outwards by the action of being towed through the water. Boats driven by steam engines had much more power than sailing trawlers and so were able to tow heavier nets with the potential to cause damage to the spawning grounds.

In the early years of the twentieth century there were a number of sailing trawlers at work in the lough, based at Rathmullan, Lehardan, Buncrana and Fahan. They fished mainly in the sandy inner part of the lough as it was believed, in those days before echo sounders, that the rough sea bottom north of Swilly Rocks would tear the trawl to pieces. However, from the 1920s onward, younger, more adventurous, fishermen equipped with the new petrol/paraffin internal combustion engines in their boats proved that it was possible to find tracks through the rough ground. Of course these areas were very productive as they had previously only been fished with lines. It was much easier to capture fish with a trawl than to entice them onto a hook! With an engine, a much smaller boat had the same catching power as a larger vessel, leading to savings in crew numbers, capital outlay and maintenance. The sailing trawlers gave way to the new technology of the day.

The period 1939–45 was a bonanza for the trawlers of the Swilly. Steam trawlers from Fleetwood and other English ports were unable to fish the offshore Donegal

grounds, as they had done for many years, because of the U-boat menace. The result was that fish stocks boomed in a very short space of time and it seemed no matter how hard the small trawlers worked, fish became ever more plentiful. The sheltered nature of the lough meant that very few days were lost due to bad weather. Britain needed food, especially protein, and the UK Government introduced a transport subsidy to encourage Ireland to export food to the industrial centres of England, Wales and Scotland. For the first time, the Swilly fishermen had access to major markets with no cost for transport. Agents were appointed by the British government to co-ordinate the buying and transport of fish. Prices were sky high – a 7 stone (43kg) box of haddock sold for 30*s*. For comparison, in Killybegs in 1970, a year of reasonable prices, a 7 stone box of haddock was still selling at 30*s*.!

After 1945 some fishermen invested their earnings in bigger, fully decked boats of up to 50 feet. With these vessels they were no longer confined to the lough but could brave the open seas to take advantage of the fish stocks that lay to seaward. These boats periodically fished from ports as far away as Kilkeel and Howth on the east coast and Killybegs on the west coast. However, no fisherman moved his centre of operations permanently to one of the major ports – they all kept their homes on the Swilly. Today very few trawlers are based around the lough, one of the last was sold from Inch Island a couple of years ago. Visiting Greencastle boats are scarce on the Swilly now too, as a result of EU policy and quotas.

8.2 Fishing boats off Urris pier, Leannan Bay. Photo: Nigel McDowell.

Most whitefishing is done now by well-equipped halfdeckers, mainly tangle netting for skate, a generic term that includes the ray species. Thornback, blonde and cuckoo are the most common skates and rays caught. They come inshore in great numbers in May to lay their egg cases in shallow water, leaving in late July. The newly hatched young may be seen feeding on the food rich banks in late summer, leaving to follow their parents when they are strong enough to face the open sea. Tangle nets consist of a line of large mesh netting set on the sea bottom. As the fish forage for food they come against the net and get tangled up. The mesh size of the netting is chosen so that smaller fish can pass safely through.

Shellfishing

The halfdecker fleet now count shellfish as their mainstay. The boats at Leannan started to fish crab in the early 1970s in the outer part of the lough and now roam up to twenty miles offshore in search of their prey. The best time for crab fishing is from August onwards as they get into condition for breeding. Peak condition coincides nicely with peak consumer demand in France and Spain in the weeks running up to Christmas when vivier lorries (lorries with salt water tanks) take live crabs in tanks of continually oxygenated seawater directly to the continental

8.3 A collection of lobster pots, Leannan Bay.
Photo: Nigel McDowell.

markets. The fishermen select the crabs extremely carefully, as weak or diseased specimens quickly die from stress, and could cause the loss of others in the same tank.

Lobsters, fished mainly in the summer months, used to be regarded as a poor man's fishing as prices were not good and fishing methods were very labour intensive. Pot frames had to be made from scrap timber for the bases and hazels cut for the bows. The netting cover then had to be knitted by hand including the all-important 'eye' – the spout through which the lobster crawls into the pot. Making pots was a winter-long job and limited the number any one boat could fish. The pots had to be baited with small fish and set close to the rocky shoreline where the lobsters lived but if there was a sudden gale, all a fisherman's pots could be lost or destroyed in a single night.

Much has changed with the advent of metal frames and factory-produced netting. Hydraulic haulers have done away with laborious hand hauling and the discerning continental market is prepared to pay ever-higher prices for fresh, live Donegal lobster – up to £10 per kilo before the global financial crash. In the Swilly, the water is too brackish for many lobsters to live south of a line from Macamish to Ned's Point but stocks increase towards the open sea. There are also good stocks of velvet crab (*Necora puber*), especially on the west side of the lough, and they are in demand commercially, but so far they have not been targeted by pot fishermen.

For many boats, shrimps are providing a livelihood during the winter, rather than battling the open sea for crab. Most of them now fish from Fahan marina where they are safe from winter storms and can lie afloat at all times. This is a far cry from their grandfather's daily toil of launching and pulling up, loading and unloading, digging boats into nests and tying them down in bad weather. Shrimps are caught in small, plastic, baited pots. These work best when free to move with

8.4 Lobster pots made with
more modern materials,
Leannan Bay. Photo:
Nigel McDowell.

the motion of the water, simulating the movements of the seaweed, where the shrimps like to live. The market for shrimps is the same as for lobster and crab, and the same care must be exercised in selecting specimens for shipping. On the day when the French or Spanish lorry comes it is wonderful to see big, hard-handed fishermen handling tiny shrimp with such loving care!

There is no record of mussels being harvested in the Swilly in earlier years, either for sale or for domestic consumption. It is hard to believe that such an abundant food source was neglected – perhaps there were plenty of superior alternatives. In the winter of 1986, however, there was a shortage of mussels in the UK and merchants came to the Swilly asking fishermen to harvest the abundant natural beds north of Inch Island. A 'Klondike' ensued with boats from as far away as Malin Head making the most of the opportunity to earn some money at a quiet time of year. Thousands of tonnes of wild mussels were dredged up and landed at Buncrana and Inch Island. Timing was critical as the beds could only be accessed by boat for a few hours at high water and the mussels had then to be landed before the tide left the landing places. For some fishermen fishing wild mussels during the winter quiet time has now developed into the alternative enterprise of mussel aquaculture.

A few fishermen tried to exploit whelks (*Buccinum undatum*) when there was great demand from Korea in the 1990s. While stocks were found off Kinnegar, near Rathmullan, and off Ray, near the Leannan Estuary, they were insufficient to maintain a specific fishery. Whelks are caught in pots made from 25-litre plastic drums with the tops cut off and replaced by a sheet of netting with a slit in it. The snail-like whelks climb up the side of the drum and fall through the slit in the net to get at the bait, which is secured in the bottom of the pot. The net at the top of the pot stops them from getting out again.

Oysters have been a feature of fishing on the Swilly for many years. In the 1800s there was a major fishery on the Ballynakilly shoals west of Inch Island but the stocks were overfished and have never recovered in that area. All that is left is a mass of dead oyster shell over a wide area, which gives some idea of the scale of the fishery at the time. Oysters at that time sold for 3*d*. per hundred. The Farland Channel between Inch and Burt also held good stocks of oysters and is nowadays used for the aquaculture of native oysters. When they reproduce, the spat can travel quite long distances with the tidal currents and, if it finds a suitable area to settle in, can create completely new beds. Recently oyster beds have been found south of Rathmullan all the way to the mouth of the Leannan River. There is a long-standing and productive oyster fishery just to the west of Newtown-cunningham, near Ballybegly Point, exploited by about twenty small boats using the traditional Irish dredge, an iron triangle about 3ft (1m) long with a blade on its lower edge that scrapes along the bottom and scoops the oysters into the netting bag attached to the frame. A tradition of hand gathering of oysters exists among some families in the Ball Green area, near Ramelton. Conflict has arisen between fishers of native oysters (*Ostrea edulis*) and aquaculture interests because the same areas of seabed are prime spots for both activities.

Salmon Fishing

From the 1950s until 2006 the main quarry for Swilly fishermen was salmon. In the spring, Atlantic salmon (*Salmo salar*) make their way from their winter feeding grounds off Greenland towards the Faeroe Islands and down the west coast of Scotland to the rivers of their birth. Although the peak season was mainly during June and July the abundance of salmon and the prices paid combined to allow the fishermen to earn the bulk of their annual income during this period. Draft netting consists of deploying ('shooting') a semicircle of net from a suitable sandy shore near the mouth of a river. When the net was pulled in it contained any salmon that had been swimming towards the river. In popular fishing spots, crews have to wait their turn to shoot their nets, which can give rise to frayed tempers if the salmon are running well. Salmon do not arrive neatly spread out over the season. Rain coming down from the river will make them more anxious to enter it whereas dry weather will make them lie back. Calm weather may make them stay at sea in deeper water; the draft net fisherman has to wait for the salmon to come to him — sometimes a frustrating business. When they do come, the fisherman may need to work 24 hours a day if needs be. Then the weekly legal close time (no fishing) from 0600 on Saturday morning until 0600 on Monday morning must be observed in order to guarantee enough salmon safe passage up the river to spawn. The most popular areas for draft netting are near the mouth of the Crana River at Porthaw and on the Leannan Estuary.

A very ancient form of salmon netting is practised in the River Swilly near Letterkenny. It is known as 'loop netting' and consists of a large frame about 15ft long and tapering from 6ft to 4ft deep. A loose bag of netting is fastened to the frame that is held upright in the water across the current by the fisherman. The netting flows back with the current to form a bag. Any salmon moving along with the current passes through the upright frame and is trapped in the bag of netting. Using this method, many hours are spent standing up to the waist in cold water, possibly for small returns.

Drift netting for salmon has been practised for many years from drontheims, sailing and rowing fairly close to the coast. The advent of engines in the 1920s meant that fishermen could venture further to sea instead of waiting for the salmon to come to them. The cotton or hemp nets had to be landed and dried daily to prevent them from rotting. These nets only caught salmon at night when the fish could not see them. Even so, on calm nights salmon refused to mesh in the nets. It took a little wind to oxygenate the surface of the water and stir the salmon into action. This meant that fishermen tried to stay at sea in as much weather as possible – a dangerous occupation in an open boat with a low-powered engine.

The new nylon nets introduced in the 1960s did not have to be dried every day and their smaller bulk meant that boats could carry more nets, leading to an increase in salmon landings. With the introduction of nets made from finer twines in the late 1970s fishermen discovered that they could catch salmon in daylight, initially in rough weather and then, as netting technology progressed, fish were captured even on relatively calm days. In the old days of night fishing there were only about three hours of darkness; now fishing could take place twenty-four-hours a day.

Salmon stocks have, however, declined for various reasons. Successive governments failed to enforce the laws designed to protect the stocks. This stock decline was likely exacerbated by drainage and forestry schemes, which damaged the spawning beds, and other environmental factors affecting the survival and growth of young salmon at sea. In an effort to restore and preserve salmon the Irish government finally banned drift netting for salmon in 2007, and a way of life that had sustained generations of fishermen was gone.

Fishing Boats and Boatbuilding

The typical boat used for herring fishing in the Swilly was the 'drontheim', so called because they were originally imported from Trondheim in Norway. They were double-ended, clinker-built traditional Scandinavian multi-purpose boats bearing a strong resemblance to a Viking longship. Propulsion was by three or four pairs of oars and one or two lugsails, a very simple sailing rig. Eventually 'kit boats' were imported, consisting of the keel, stem and sternpost, which were then finished off by local boatbuilders. In time, Donegal builders learned how to construct the complete boat, adding features that made them more suitable for local conditions. With the addition of engines, these vessels have become the well-known 'halfdeckers' that are still used extensively for salmon and lobster fishing around the coast.

8.5 *Fisher Boy*, a typical Lough Swilly halfdecker built by John Flanagan of Buncrana, 1981. Photo: John Niven.

8.6 *Fisher Boy* and *North Star*, halfdeckers owned by John and Robert Niven, respectively. This 1985 photograph gives a good view of the boats from bow and stern. Photo: John Niven.

Rathmullan had the biggest concentration of fishing boats and boatbuilders in the Swilly. From the 1800s and possibly earlier boats were built not only for Lough Swilly owners but also for crews in west Donegal, a tradition that continues today. Many places that now have no sign of commercial fishing were at this time important centres for the herring industry – Doagh Beg, Portsalon and Killygarvan on the west side, Port Ban (Dunree) and the mouth of the River Crana on the east side. There were no piers or harbours in those days; the boats had to be emptied of the catch, nets, oars, sails and ballast and these were then hauled up on the shore for safety until the next trip, a backbreaking task for men tired and wet after a night's fishing in an open boat with no shelter and no means of making hot food or drink. The fishermen would dig out 'nests' for the boats above the shoreline to

8.7 The trawler *Rival* at
Rathmullan pier, 2009.
Photo: Andrew Cooper.

protect them from winter storms. It is still possible to see them around the lough;
there are two at the north end of Port Ban that are quite accessible.

Rathmullan regatta, established in the nineteenth century, gave fishermen and
their families a break from routine and an opportunity to test their skills and
strength against crews from other areas around the lough. There were sailing and
rowing races specifically for fishermen, some for fishing boats and others for boats
built specially for racing. These hotly contested races were a matter of pride and
honour for the fishermen and their supporters from the homeports and townlands.
Winning boats and crews often had poems and songs composed to celebrate the
occasion.

The versatile halfdecker has made the transition to other fisheries, as it has done
many times in the past, proving that the fishermen's trust in this tough little
workhorse is well placed. Continuing in the tradition of drontheim builders of
earlier years, many sturdy halfdeckers were built for the Swilly and also west
Donegal by a self-taught boatbuilder from Buncrana, John Flanagan, before his
untimely death in 1981. Rossreagh Boatyard near Ramelton still provides an
invaluable repair and modernization service to fishermen and yachtsmen alike.
There is also a long tradition of fishermen who are as skilled at repairing and
maintaining their boats as they are at fishing.

The Browns: A Lough Swilly Fishing Family

The Browns of Inch Island are one of the best-known fishing families on Lough
Swilly, and are typical of many who earned their living from the sea. As in most

8.8 Inch and Leannan fishing boats crowded into Inch pier for shelter during a southerly blow, 1988. Photo: John Niven.

cases, there is a history of fishing that spans several generations. In 1611 John Brown, an ancestor of the present Brown family, was granted a charter by James I to establish a ferry from Fahan to Rathmullan. The family tradition of running the ferry along with fishing and boatbuilding continued until recent years. The charter is held in the Public Record Office, Kew, London.

In the mid-1800s, possibly around the time of the Famine, James Brown went to America and worked on steamboats on the Great Lakes. One of his fellow crewmen, a Native American, was extensively scalded by a steam leak from the ship's boilers. James threw him into the ship's flour chest in the galley, preventing further fluid loss and thereby saving his life. For this he was made a blood brother at a tribal ceremony. When James came back to live in Inch Island in the late 1800s he resumed the family occupations of fishing, ferrying and boatbuilding. He sawed whole trees by hand into the planks he needed, assisted by James Boyle from another Inch fishing family. In common with other Swilly boatbuilders he took orders for new boats from west Donegal crews.

It is said that in late August these crews walked from their homes to Rathmullan and were ferried over to Fahan by James, placing their order for the new boat at the same time. They then took the train to Derry and travelled to Glasgow on the 'Scotch boat'. After working at the 'tattie hoking' or potato harvest they returned to Inch Island where James had their boat ready and they paid for it with their earnings from Scotland. The crew then sailed and rowed their new boat out of the Swilly and westward to their home port in time to take part in the winter herring fishing. However, one boat disappeared with its crew on the delivery trip and it is said that after this event James never built another new drontheim. He lived in a cottage on the foreshore at Jeremy's Point but later moved to a cottage he built at Lacken Point. The tarred felt roof of the cottage was the most expensive part of

8.9 The motor fishing
vessel *Shenandoah*,
registered in Sligo (SO606),
and owned by the Brown
family of Inch Island, 1972.
Photo: John Niven.

the house so he moved it to the new dwelling by getting six strong neighbours to
lift it bodily, walk it to the new location and set it down on the prepared walls.
James was adventurous and quick witted; on one occasion while fishing herring in
his drontheim a gale sprang up and his crew became concerned for their safety.
Both wind and tide were against them so James knew the best option was to stay
attached to the nets as a sea anchor until the tide turned and took them back to
Inch. He said 'Listen, boys, I'm as fond of my life as you are of yours so don't
worry until you see me panicking' and with that lay down in the bottom of the boat
and went to sleep! The tide duly turned and they got back home safely.

The drontheim *Violet* used by the Brown family from this time until the 1980s
is now in the Greencastle Maritime Museum. James married Sarah Hodge, also
from the island, and they had one son, also called James. He followed in his father's
footsteps but had a strong interest in horticulture, making the best use of his small
plot of land. There is a sod dyke around it, which was built by some shipwrecked
sailors in return for their keep in the Brown household while they were waiting to
travel home. James Jr's wife, Anne, kept a cow and hens, which went together well
with James' potatoes and vegetables. When fishing was slack in the spring he
bought herring to sell around the island from the Scotch drifters berthed in
Buncrana.

James and Anne had four sons and a daughter born between 1910 and 1920. The
boys were very keen on the new engines and the family soon began converting
drontheims into motor boats. Sadly, Johnny, the eldest boy, was drowned in Fahan
Channel in 1926. The remaining three sons worked their way up to bigger and
more seaworthy boats, fishing herring and whitefish as far afield as Downings,
Bunbeg, Kincasslagh and Portnoo. When the boys were away Violet helped her
father row and sail the ferry for the all-important cash income. Violet and Maggie
Hardy, another fisherman's daughter from Inch, often won the women's rowing
race at Rathmullan regatta. During the 1939–45 period, the Browns, in common
with other Swilly fishermen, capitalized on the abundant fish stocks and good

prices created by wartime food scarcity. In late 1945 they were able to buy the *Girl Christina*, a 40ft fully decked Scottish fishing boat, which had just been released from British Admiralty service. With the earnings from this boat they then bought the 45ft *Shenandoah* and the 35ft *Leonorah*. These boats fished periodically from Killybegs as well as the Swilly area, seine netting[1] for whitefish and ring netting for herring. The smaller halfdeckers were still used for salmon driftnetting as it was thought that the bigger boats were too unwieldy and uneconomic for this fishery.

In 1957 Jim and Bertie Brown along with their crewmen Tom Porter and Eugene McGinley were drowned while salmon fishing when their boat, the *Playmate*, drifted onto the rocky coast just west of Fanad Head. This devastated the family and left Willie, their remaining brother, to carry on with his sons. Around the 1980s the change was made to bottom trawling for whitefish and midwater trawling for herring. Along with drifting for salmon, sea angling trips and the new mussel fishing, the lough continued to yield a good living for the Brown family. Although the ferry was no longer viable on a daily basis it still attracted huge crowds on the day of Rathmullan regatta.

Today, Alan and Kenny Brown farm mussels around Inch Island, Dermot and Gavin Brown continue to trawl for whitefish and herring. Fishing is as unpredictable as ever but the Browns are experienced in moving quickly and exploiting whatever opportunities present themselves for wresting a living from the sea.

---

1 Seine nets are long flat nets like a fence that are weighted at the bottom. They are used to encircle a shoal of fish.

Chapter 9

Aquaculture in Lough Swilly

Joanne Gaffney

Introduction

Aquaculture is a food production sector that has grown dramatically in the last half century, though it is an activity that has been practised for centuries, perhaps as far back as 2500 BC in China. Modern aquaculture has seen an average worldwide growth rate of 8.8% since 1970, compared with only 1.2% for capture fisheries and 2.8% for terrestrial animal production systems during the same period.

With a global production of nearly 52 million tonnes in 2006 world aquaculture has increased by one third since the beginning of the millennium. The EU-27 aquaculture industry produced about 1.3 million tonnes of fish, shellfish and crustaceans in 2006, representing a turnover of €3 billion and approximately 65,000 jobs. The industry has stagnated in recent years, due among other reasons to the reduced availability of suitable culture sites because of the ever-increasing competition between vying stakeholder interests in the coastal zone.

Irish aquaculture produce is mainly exported to meet the worldwide demand for marine and freshwater food. The modern Irish aquaculture industry began in the 1970s and it has experienced significant challenges in the last few years. In 2007, the total production volume of the shellfish and finfish aquaculture sectors was 48,350 tonnes, with a value of €105.7 million, providing employment for 1,981 people. For 2009 Lough Swilly produced 4500–5000 tonnes of aquaculture products with a combined value in the region of €8.5 million. Irish aquaculture, however, remains poorly understood by the general public and in many cases people have no idea of the species farmed or the production methods employed in their own areas. This chapter describes the diverse aquaculture activities in Lough Swilly, which has become one of the major centres of aquaculture in Ireland.

Aquaculture in Lough Swilly

Aquaculture in Lough Swilly focuses on the production of three species for both processing and fresh markets: salmon (*Salmo salar*), blue mussels (*Mytilus edulis*) and Pacific oysters (*Crassostrea gigas*).

MUSSEL FARMING

The blue mussel, a native species, has been cultivated in Ireland for about 30 years. Mussel farming is now well established throughout the country with farms located in many bays and inlets, where there are also naturally occurring populations.

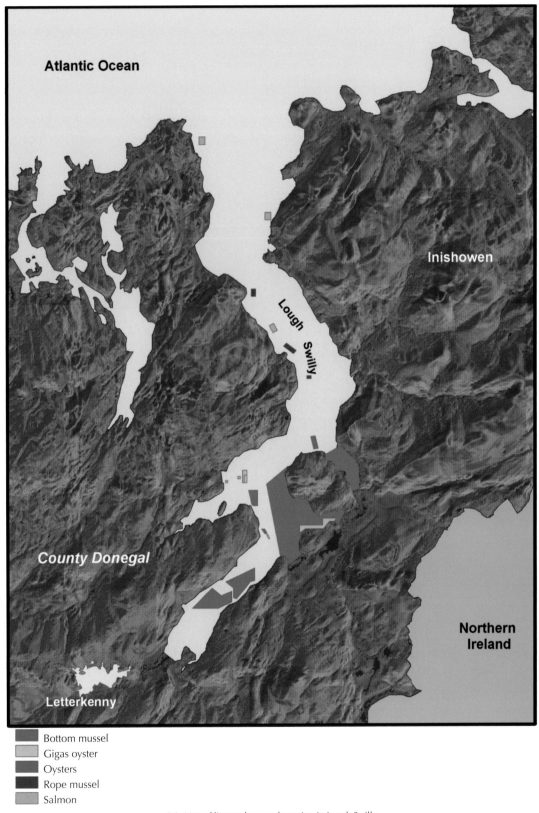

Atlantic Ocean

Inishowen

Lough
Swilly

County Donegal

Northern
Ireland

Letterkenny

Bottom mussel
Gigas oyster
Oysters
Rope mussel
Salmon

9.1 Map of licensed aquaculture sites in Lough Swilly.

9.2 Mussel cultivation on the western shore of Lough Swilly. Photo: Emmett Johnston.

Their natural habitat is on rocky surfaces or muddy bottoms where they aggregate together tightly. Bottom grown mussel farming in Ireland has developed rapidly over the last twenty years. It is a form of extensive culture, a type of fish farming where the producer has limited control over the factors that affect the species to be farmed. The sector developed in its initial phase using imported second-hand mussel dredgers to fish for juvenile mussels known as 'seed' primarily in the Irish Sea. These vessels were originally designed for use in the sheltered waters of the Netherlands and were not well suited to fishing in open sea conditions. The introduction of the EU safety regulations for sea fishing vessels, known as the 'Torremolinos Protocol', brought about the forced obsolescence of many of these second-hand vessels, as the cost of upgrading them was prohibitive. Producers had to invest in modern vessels in order to secure access to juvenile mussel fishery areas in the Irish Sea.

Bottom grown mussel farming has been conducted in Lough Swilly since the early 1980s. Farming began through a cooperative approach, but some individuals have since developed their own specific interests in aquaculture and have even diversified into different species.

In the case of Lough Swilly juvenile mussels known as 'seed' are transferred from naturally occurring wild seed mussel beds to culture plots/licensed areas where conditions are more favourable, growth and survival rates are improved and the stock can be managed more effectively. The 'seed' is relayed directly onto the seabed and thus there is no need for any growing equipment apart from the fishing vessel. Most of the beds are sub-tidal and therefore many people are unaware that these farms even exist.

Dredging, a common form of fishing, is used for harvesting bivalve molluscs such as oysters, clams and scallops from the seabed. A dredge is a metal-framed

basket with a bottom of connected iron rings or wire netting called a chain belly. The lower edge of the frame has a raking bar, with or without teeth, depending upon the species targeted. Mussel vessels in Ireland most commonly use between two and four dredges. The types of dredge used are 2m-wide mussel dredges with a flat bar and a smooth curtain over the chain belly that is designed to skim the surface of the sea bed and separate mussels from the underlying substrate. Mussels are filter feeders, that is, they feed by filtering naturally occurring particulate matter from the water. Mussels will then excrete undigested waste matter or digested faecal matter from their body cavity. This faecal matter (pseudofaeces) quickly accumulates and develops into a layer of mud (known as 'mussel mud'). To harvest the animals, the mussel dredge tows through this mussel mud layer between the shellfish and the substrate and thus does not invade the original sea floor.

The culture of mussels on the seabed is not the only form of mussel culture trialled in Lough Swilly; there have been a number of trials of suspended culture systems. This culture method involves placing a settlement medium (rope) in the water column, on which juvenile mussels settle. The naturally collected mussel seed is then placed in mesh stockings, which are suspended from floating rope long-lines in the water column of the on-growing areas. As with bottom mussel farming,

9.3 Mussels are harvested by dredging, the evidence of which is visible here in the lines on the seabed. Photo: Emmett Johnston.

9.4 Oyster farming on the inter-tidal flats of the eastern shore. Photo: Emmett Johnston.

mussels cultured using suspended culture techniques obtain their food by filtering microscopic algae from the water. Within 9–18 months, thin shelled, sand-free mussels with high meat contents can be harvested. While the cultivation of mussels using a suspended culture system has been very successful in many bays throughout Ireland, including the neighbouring Mulroy Bay, this activity has yet to develop to a commercial scale in Lough Swilly mainly as a result of the exposed nature of the sites in the outer area of the lough.

OYSTER FARMING

Two species of oyster are cultured in Lough Swilly – the native oyster (*Ostrea edulis*) and the Pacific oyster (*Crassostrea gigas*), with the culture of Pacific oysters dominating production in the lough as it does all over Europe.

While Pacific oysters have been cultured in Ireland for about twenty-five years, oyster farming within Lough Swilly only commenced in the early 1990s. Oyster farming in the Swilly is a form of intensive culture carried out in the inter-tidal zone. Cultivation of the Pacific oyster is carried out by growing the oysters in bags placed on trestles. Trestles are metal frames measuring 3m x 1m that stand 0.4m in height and hold five bags each. Bags are made of a plastic mesh and are fastened to trestles using rubber straps. Bags vary in mesh size depending on oyster stock grade (4mm, 7mm, 9mm, 14mm). The production cycle begins in the lough when seed is introduced from a hatchery (usually in France or Guernsey) in the spring of each year. The seed is placed in the mesh plastic bags at densities of around 1,000 per bag. The bags are shaken on site a minimum of three times over the growing season. The densities are reduced as the biomass increases in the bags. Finishing densities are approximately 15–20 individual oysters per bag to ensure maximum quality.

Sites are accessed at low tide using a tractor and trailer and more recently by the use of purpose-built flat bottom barges. Farms within Lough Swilly are positioned between Mean High Water Neap and Mean Low Water Spring, allowing 2.5 to 3.5 hours exposure depending on prevailing weather conditions. This translates to approximately 15% visual exposure during daylight hours over a typical month. Onshore farm work activities include trestle deployment, bag shaking, bag removal and replacement, bag turning and general farm maintenance. As with mussel farming, oysters are filter feeders, and thus require the addition of no feed or chemicals during the growth cycle.

SALMON FARMING

The only salmon farming operation in Lough Swilly is that of Marine Harvest Ireland. The company was set up in 1979 as Fanad Fisheries, having been founded by a group of Irish shareholders led by Anthony Fox, who had up to then been a biology teacher in Dublin. Starting out as a sea trout farm, the operation soon changed to salmon farming. In 1981, a 50:50 joint venture was established with A/S MOWI, a company based in Bergen, Norway. This strengthened the Irish operation by providing access to stock, technology and finance. The company has operated a salmon (*Salmo salar*) production site at Anny Point on the western side of Lough Swilly since 1985. The annual licensed capacity of this site is 1,000 tonnes of salmon. The site is serviced from a shore base at Scraggy Bay.

Marine Harvest Ireland is a fully integrated salmon farm. This means that it carries out all phases of the business, starting with taking the ova from broodstock to packaging the final product of fresh salmon ready for consumers. Marine Harvest Ireland's business involves three main products. The company sells: (i) disease-free fertilized ova to other farms around the world; (ii) Organic Atlantic salmon, under the Organic Salmon Co. brand; and (iii) Premium Eco-Label Atlantic salmon, under the Donegal Silver brand. Both the organic salmon and premium Eco-Label salmon are distributed in Ireland, Europe and North America.

The production cycle starts in freshwater hatcheries where ova are stripped and fertilized from broodstock fish from Mulroy Bay in early winter, typically November. These ova are then incubated very carefully until the eyes of the fish embryo become clearly visible through the transparent eggshell. Fertilized or eyed ova are quite robust and can be handled and shipped to other farms and hatcheries. The company employs its own geneticist, and maintains a strong link with Trinity College and Stirling University among others. As the production cycle continues, eyed ova are laid down in hatchery troughs where further incubation leads to hatching at which stage the 'alevin' (tiny salmon) emerges from ova. Alevins are not unlike tadpoles in appearance. They are very small fish with a distinct and relatively large yolk sac, which contains its nourishment for a further 4 to 6 weeks. Once this yolk sac is absorbed, the alevin has reached the stage to start feeding, typically coinciding with the rising temperatures in spring.

This so-called 'first feeding' stage is one of the most critical and delicate stages in the production cycle where excellent husbandry skills and high standards of hygiene are essential. Once they begin to feed, the fish are referred to as 'fry'. These fry grow rapidly in the various circular tanks of the hatchery. The hatcheries draw water from nearby lakes chosen for their pure waters and low incidence of wild migratory fish, which could potentially be a source of disease to the farmed stocks.

Marine Harvest Ireland has two large hatcheries – one at Procklis, Falcarragh, where the unit draws water from Lough Altan, a large lake between Mount Errigal and Aghla More, and a second at Pettigo drawing its water from Lough Derg. In these hatcheries, the fry grow into smolts at which stage the young salmon is ready to go to sea. As the fish smoltifies, it turns silver. Once smoltification is completed, this physiological change enables the fish to cope with the high level of salt in seawater. Smoltification takes place in spring, some 14 months after the ova first hatched. The altering of light and darkness during smolt production can be used to influence the time at which the fish are ready to go to sea. This helps smolt units spread their production and delivery, and ultimately also helps to provide for a more continuous availability of salmon for the consumer. Marine Harvest Ireland produces both spring and autumn smolts.

The Donegal seawater sites are supplied with smolt from the Altan smolt unit. Once at sea the smolts are reared in nets suspended from circular floating structures known as pens. These are moored in groups in locations where there are strong water flows in order to provide the stock with optimum environmental conditions. Salmon are extremely sensitive to pollution and do not grow if their water is not clean and well oxygenated. This fundamental requirement means that a salmon farm can only produce the amount that can be infinitely sustained by the environment in which it operates. Consequently, the monitoring of both fish and environment is a very important aspect of salmon farming. For this reason, only the outer Swilly is regarded as suitable for salmon farming because of various water inputs into the lough south of the existing operations at Anny Point.

One of the key success factors for salmon aquaculture is the control of disease, which in turn relies on good health management. The Swilly fish farm operator has its own laboratory to assist with this, and all salmonid movements are tightly regulated. Feed for salmon farms is sourced from non-quota marine fishes as well as corn and soya crops. The efficient conversion of feed (1.1kg of feed produces 1.0kg of salmon) arises primarily from fish being cold blooded so that, unlike their agricultural counterparts, no energy is required to maintain body temperature. As feed costs can make up close to 60% of salmon production costs, feeding is the most important daily task – 365 days of the year. This task is increasingly supported with

9.5 Covered salmon cages near the mouth of the lough. Photo: Nigel McDowell.

sophisticated technology ranging from automatic feeders, underwater cameras and lights, as well as computer systems to monitor trends in appetite and performance.

The production cycle at sea from a smolt of *c*.50g to a 2–5kg salmon takes between 18 and 20 months. Once the fish have reached the desired weight they are transferred to the harvest station in Mulroy Bay where they are slaughtered as rapidly and with as little stress as possible. This is vitally important for animal welfare as well as for quality reasons. They are immediately chilled and processed. The organic and Eco-Label salmon is processed at Rinmore, from where they are distributed to Ireland, Europe and North America.

Sustainability

The aquaculture sector is tightly regulated in terms of site location, site management, environmental performance, animal welfare, aquatic animal health and human health. In addition, with the increased consumer focus on the issues of environment and sustainability, many companies now voluntarily subscribe to higher production and environmental performance in the form of eco,[1] quality and organic standards. The sector has further been the subject of a recent communication from the European Commission, which focuses on the means of building a sustainable future for aquaculture in member states. This communication aims to increase awareness among policy makers and public bodies, about the importance of aquaculture in the European Union, while also providing EU leadership and guidance to stakeholders and administrations to ensure consistency and clarity in designing policies for the sustainable development of European aquaculture.

---

1 Eco-standards are indicators of responsible environmental practice.

9.6 Uncovered salmon cages.
Photo: Nigel McDowell.

Aquaculture requires water of the highest quality to guarantee the health of aquatic animals and safe and high quality products. Recognition of this led to the drafting of the Directive on the protection of the quality of Shellfish Growing Waters, which places strict water quality parameters on discharges to areas where shellfish are cultured. This Directive will be repealed and incorporated into the Water Framework Directive (WFD) in 2015. The Commission has stated though, that measures under the WFD shall, as a minimum, maintain the present protection level of shellfish growing areas as afforded by this Directive.

The EU has also stated that the sector would benefit from an improved framework for governance and a current challenge is to improve the image of aquaculture. Key to this aim will be an ability to operate under optimal husbandry conditions, incorporating good health and adequate feed suited to the physiological needs of the farmed aquatic animals.

Aquaculture Management

Aquaculture development in Lough Swilly faces a number of challenges in response to which a Co-ordinated Local Aquaculture Management Systems (CLAMS) group has been established. The unique CLAMS process is an all-Ireland initiative that seeks to manage the development of aquaculture in bays and inshore waters at a local level. In each case, the plan seeks to align aquaculture interests with relevant national and local government policies and plans. This process has been widely adopted in bays and inshore waters where aquaculture is practised around the Irish coast.

Aquaculture Initiative EEIG

The Cross-Border Aquaculture Initiative EEIG (CBAIT) was formed in 1998. It is a European Economic Interest Grouping, established as a joint venture between Northern Ireland and the Republic of Ireland. An Bord Iascaigh Mhara (BIM) and Northern Ireland Seafood (NIS) act as the main shareholders with additional board representatives from both DAFF (formally DCMNR) and DARD (the two departments with responsibility for the implementation of government policy as it relates to aquaculture) and the lough's Agency. The Initiative commenced operations in 1999 and is headquartered in Dundalk, Co. Louth, with sub offices in Downpatrick, Co. Down.

The Aquaculture Initiative operates in the six border counties of the Republic of Ireland and Northern Ireland. It provides advice and assistance regarding financial, technical, environmental, quality and strategic matters in order to provide effective support to both new and existing aquaculture ventures in the eligible area. It is uniquely positioned to provide a range of support services for the sustainable development of the aquaculture industry in the cross border area. The Aquaculture Initiative provides support and a liaison officer to the Lough Swilly Coordinated Local Aquaculture Management (CLAMS) Group.

Chapter 10

Marine Tourism and Recreation

Jessica Hodgson

> I wish I could catch a wave
> and ride it to the shore.
> A wave with a silver mane
> tossing in the wind,
> an arched neck
> of turquoise marble, melting.
> I wish I could tame it
> with whispers,
> feel its spittle on my face,
> taste the salt of its sweat,
> become one being with it
> in an explosion of white
> crashing on the sand,
> breaking to a bubbling,
> a susurrating shine

'Riding the Wave' by Clare McDonnell,
inspired by Lough Swilly.

Introduction

Like many places in Donegal, Lough Swilly and its shores are special for various reasons – its people, culture, environment and maybe even the weather. For the people who use it, the lough is valuable from many perspectives – work, play, social and mental well-being. The most important commercial activity in Lough Swilly is primarily associated with tourism; revenue and jobs are generated by accommodation, pubs, restaurants, local shops, and marine and coastal recreation providers. Many of the businesses in the Lough Swilly catchment area are built on its natural and built resources and the habitats it provides for wildlife. This chapter explores modern marine recreation and tourism activities in and around Lough Swilly.

A 1987 study carried out on behalf of the Sheephaven, Fanad, Mulroy and Rosguill Development Co-operative, found that participation in water sports on Lough Swilly was almost entirely confined to tourists with only two exceptions – Sheephaven Sub Aqua Club and Fahan Yacht Club. Tourists brought their own equipment (canoes, boats, windsurfing equipment) and there was only one centre

10.1 Beach visitors at Portsalon find a wide, uncrowded beach. Photo: Nigel McDowell.

in the Swilly area exploiting water sports on a commercial basis (Fahan Yacht Club). Portsalon, Rathmullan, Fahan and Ballywhoriskey were all identified in the report as good locations for water sports activities. It was suggested that the region could support a centre offering water-based activity holidays with potential to combine other activities such as hill-walking, orienteering and mountaineering.

In the 1980s, however, there was little surplus money for pleasure sports or equipment and consequently progressing marine tourism and recreation was difficult. Some activities were deemed elitist, for example, sailing, and there was scepticism that tourism and recreation could provide an alternative to commercial activities in textiles and agriculture, which tended to dominate the area.

The apparent affluence of the 90s and noughties changed attitudes towards outdoor activities and water sports. More disposable income, access to information via the internet and, a perception at least, of more free time, meant environmental awareness increased and conservation became a popular cause.

Awareness of the impacts of climate change and lower emission activity is being encouraged by government and there is a definite push to change the way we live, from that of a 'disposable' psyche to one of recycling and conservation. This, from a marine tourism perspective, opens the door to ecotourism and passive water sports.

Lough Swilly with its stunning scenery provides an ideal setting for many outdoor activities. In this regard it is a playground surrounded by cliffs, unspoilt

10.2 The beach at Rathmullan is host to a range of visitor activities. Photo: Nigel McDowell.

beaches, calm, safe swimming locations and numerous wrecks for angling and diving. Activities that existed at the time of the 1987 study continue and there has been some growth in the tourism industry.

Recreational Activities in and around Lough Swilly

BEACHES

Lough Swilly has many beaches; some are hidden in secret coves and inlets around the coast while others are long stretches of golden sand that go on for miles. For many coastal towns and villages the beach is the centre of activity and a valued resource. The most popular beaches around Lough Swilly are managed by Donegal County Council and have gained either Blue Flag (Lisfannon and Portsalon) or Green Coast awards (Rathmullan).

According to a survey carried out in 1998 by the University of Ulster visitors to Lisfannon tend to be frequent day trippers, the majority of whom come from within a 15-mile radius. The most popular activities at Lisfannon were picnicking, walking and exercising pets. In the same survey, Portsalon was also found to be popular for repeat visits, but a high percentage of visitors surveyed were not local and stayed overnight, mostly in local caravan parks. The most popular activities at Portsalon were walking and relaxing. It is unlikely that these trends have changed dramatically over time.

Unfortunately dumping and litter disposal are also popular activities at many beaches around Lough Swilly and it is an ongoing management challenge for the County Council given the expansive coastal area it manages. Visitors are encouraged to take their litter home with them as otherwise it ends up being a feast for seagulls, who like to throw their food around.

10.3 Digging in the sand remains a popular beach pastime. Photo: Andrew Cooper.

Good weather, especially at the weekend, can cause some traffic congestion but all beaches mentioned above have lifeguards, car parking and toilet facilities in peak season. Bye laws were introduced on these beaches in 2009 to manage the wide-ranging activities that take place there. Access to other more secluded beaches may not be so easy and may require landowner permission in some cases; it is always advisable to check with locals to ensure an area is safe for swimming.

The many beautiful unspoiled beaches are also fantastic walking locations at any time of year and are ideal for nature watching. Many other activities including dog-walking, kite-surfing and horse-riding take place on the beaches. Two horse-riding stables (Inch Island Stables and Golden Sands Equestrian Centre) are based there and use beaches in their itineraries. There is a mixture of challenging 9 hole and 18 hole golf links dotted around the coast (Otway, Portsalon, Buncrana, North West), all of which are close to safe swimming areas and services.

SCENIC AND HERITAGE ROUTES

Depending on which side of Lough Swilly is being explored access to the coast will involve travelling along one of the two spectacular drives: Fanad Drive and the Inishowen 100. Both of these routes provide stunning views with numerous vantage points and photo opportunities. The Knockalla Hill climb (part of Fanad drive on the way to Portsalon) provides a spectacular white-knuckle section of the Donegal Rally. The Rally brings with it participants, support crews and spectators that contribute directly to the local economy. The breath-taking views from the course are transmitted far and wide via the media, and this kind of publicity is very valuable. The Knockalla route, though very challenging, is also popular with cyclists.

Cyclists can also experience the east of Lough Swilly by travelling along the Inishowen cycleway. This route offers a 55km-cycle route through Derry and Donegal. The route passes by Inch Levels and Blanket Nook sites and also takes in An Grianán Aileach. The route connects to Derry via the Foyle Valley and includes Derry's city walls and Ballyarnett Country Park.

The Lough Swilly area has a rich maritime history that can be explored from these routes and by sea. Historical buildings and structures are important to the character of the area and help tell its story.

WALKING

There are numerous marked and unmarked paths by which to explore Lough Swilly. Self-guided tours are relatively safe as long as safety advice is followed. There are some lovely paths along the lough shore; Buncrana to Straghill beach is an easy stroll of 2.3km right on the lough edge. A series of sign-posted footpaths with interpretative panels and rest/picnic areas can be found outside the Fort Dunree centre to let visitors experience the stunning views and wildlife first hand.

Batt's walk in Rathmullan follows the shore along a tree-lined path and forks off into a bridal path that slopes down to the beach. This is a stunning walk in autumn when the trees change colour. It is adjacent to the Martello Tower beside the beach.

Guided walks are also available from trained and knowledgeable guides who are available to accompany groups or individuals or provide advice or information before walkers depart.

BIRDWATCHING

Lough Swilly hosts a wide variety of habitats and species and is renowned for birdwatching, especially at Inch Lake and Blanket Nook (south-east of Inch Island, approximately 9km south of Buncrana). Inch Lake is considered to be one of the largest and best examples of a shallow, low salinity lagoon in Ireland. It is a staging ground for migrating birds from three continents and provides opportunities to see the winter and spring migration of internationally significant numbers of whooper swans and greylag geese. The small island in Inch Lake supports the largest sandwich tern colony in north-west Ireland, and is an internationally important breeding colony.

The large variety of local songbirds and waterfowl provide a rich food source for native birds of prey including peregrine falcon, kestrel, merlin, sparrowhawk, buzzard, hen harrier and long-eared owl. As they are the top of the food chain, their presence demonstrates the existence of a healthy ecosystem. Due to a rich insect community endangered bats (Leisler's bat, brown long-eared bats and Pipistrelle bats) are found in the area. The Inch Levels system also has what is probably the largest population in Ireland of bearded stonewort, an endangered algae species.

Blanket Nook, a wildfowl sanctuary just a little further to the south-west of Inch Lake, has also seen an increase in both numbers and varieties of species. Large

10.4 Sea kayaking is a popular activity on Lough Swilly. Photo: Nigel McDowell.

numbers of birds commute to and from the Nook; greylag and white-fronted geese are regular visitors, and other species such as shoveler and gadwall are frequently seen.

WATER SPORTS

Beaches are also the starting point for many of the marine activities that take place on the lough. Surfing on Lough Swilly is usually limited to beginners and the north coast of Donegal is used most frequently by local surfers and schools. Only when the surf is too big elsewhere do experienced surfers use Lough Swilly (this is mainly during winter months), at Portsalon and further north.

Portsalon and Fahan are among the most popular locations in Donegal for windsurfing. Because windsurfers can launch from practically any beach or slipway, it is difficult to quantify the popularity of this sport. There does not appear to be any dedicated clubs and so it is carried out on a casual basis. The popularity of kite-surfing is also growing. Lough Swilly offers ideal conditions for beginners to medium-ability surfers because it is relatively well protected and experiences low waves. Jet skis and wake-boarders often launch from Ned's Point, Rathmullan and Portsalon slip ways.

Sea kayaking gives the explorer the opportunity to stop off at small coves and inlets and to get to places inaccessible to other boats and land-bound visitors. Kayaks launch from Leannan Bay, Fahan and White Chapel among other places. Guided tours from qualified practitioners are available from 'Just Kayak'. They provide taster sessions, coaching, white water and surf kayaking. A 4–5 day Lough Foyle to Lough Swilly circuit is also available. Kayakers often sight dolphins, basking sharks, minke whale and sun fish on this circuit. Night paddles can also be undertaken. A series of challenging kayak races take place annually in late October.

Table 10.1: Most common dive sites in Lough Swilly and off Malin Head	
Location	*General Information*
Leannan pier	Suitable for first dives and building water fitness by snorkelling. Leannan is classed as a shore dive, i.e., no boat used. Depths vary from 2 to 10m. Possible to dive there at any state of tide, though care should be taken during spring tides, when dives should take place on slack water or an incoming tide as there can be quite a localized current.
McCamish Fort	Accessed by boat, this site is almost directly opposite Ned's Point on the Knockalla coastline. Diving takes place in a small bay, directly under the fort. Water depth varies from 10 to 14m. The seabed has many large anchors dating from the First World War. It can be dived in all states of tide.
Swilly Rocks (55–17.107N 007–35.220W)	Site of the *Saldahna*, wrecked completely in a storm in January 1811. After the ship was wrecked, more than 2,000 bodies were washed ashore; nothing remains of her. There is, however, the remains of a more modern, steel wreck. This can be a great drift dive with depths varying from 1 to 20m. Great care must be taken by the boat coxswain, as there are several barely submerged rocks in the area.
Dunaff Head	A series of gullies running north/south between Dunaff Island, narrowing in the centre to an inverted keyhole swim through. General depth: 15 to 25m.
Callagh Rock	A large, solitary rock, approximately 500m on the seaward side of Dunree Fort. This dive site offers depths from 8 to 22m, with interesting gullies and boulders.
SS *Laurentic* (55–11.230N 007–35.447W)	This fantastic wreck is famous for its millions of euro worth in unrecovered gold. Mined in January 1917, this 15,000 tonne, 550ft liner is scattered over a wide area. Lying at a depth of 40m, the dive is for the more experienced diver. It can be dived in most states of tide and is ideal for practising decompression diving or mixed gasses. Buncrana was the *Laurentic's* last port of call.
Audacious	23,000 ton *Dreadnough* battleship, mined 27 October 1914. Lying upside down in 65m of water north of Lough Swilly, Co. Donegal. A huge wreck broken up by internal explosion, with 13-inch gun turrets lying on the seabed. Excellent offshore visibility with weak tidal streams, only recommended for mixed gas-divers. Massive wreck, covered in fish life.
Malin Head	Around the coast to the east from Lough Swilly; also presents a myriad of dive sites for both shore and boat dives.
RMS *Justicia*	32,000 ton White Star liner torpedoed on 20 July 1918 by UB-64. Lying in 68m of water 29 miles NW of Malin Head. Excellent offshore visibility with weak tidal streams, only recommended for mixed-gas divers.
SS *Empire Heritage*	Oil tanker torpedoed on 8 September 1944 by U-482 carrying a deck cargo of Sherman Tanks. Lying in 68m of water 18 miles NW of Malin Head. Wreck is upright, but broke her back with her cargo of tanks scattered across the seabed. Excellent offshore visibility with weak tidal streams, only recommended for mixed gas divers.

Source: Courtesy of personal comment; Inishowen Sub-Aqua Club, http://inishowensubaqua. weebly.com/; Aquaholics, https://ssl.utvinternet.com/aquaholics/dive_Locations.asp; Norsemaid Sea Enterprises Ltd, http://www.salutay.com/html/ives/scenic.htm.

Race routes vary but include Crana River around Inch Island to Rathmullan and back to Buncrana; and also the adventure race – orienteering race in a double sea kayak – Dunree to Portsalon to Crana River.

SCUBA DIVING

There are a number of scuba clubs dotted around the coast of Lough Swilly and visiting clubs and schools regularly dive in the lough. Clubs affiliated by Comhairle Fo Thionn (Irish Underwater Council) put their trainees through a thorough training process to ensure that divers are prepared for all conditions or eventualities. Accredited PADI (Professional Association of Diving Instructors) schools also use Lough Swilly.

The relatively safe and accessible waters of Lough Swilly are ideal for scuba diving and all levels can be catered for, from shallow first-time dives to more adventurous and skilled wreck dives. Powering through the water in a fast boat to the dive site and plopping overboard is a buzz to which many become addicted.

The table opposite details some of the most popular dives in Lough Swilly and also some of the more challenging dives off Malin Head to the north-east of Lough Swilly.

Diving is also a fantastic way to experience marine life and there is a chance of encountering larger mammals and fish. According to the Irish Whale and Dolphin Group a total of 586 casual sightings have been recorded in Lough Swilly from 2006 to 2009, the most common of these being bottle nose dolphins (446), harbour porpoise (82) and two whales. For the same period there were 52 casual basking shark sightings recorded.

Angling

SEA ANGLING

Sea angling doesn't require a license and Lough Swilly boasts many sites suitable for shore angling. The table below outlines locations and species available in Lough Swilly (adapted from *A guide to sea angling in the Donegal region*).

Bait can be sourced in many of the small sheltered coasts along the Swilly. Lugworm (easily noticed by the spaghetti-like mound they leave in their wake) can be dug up by trench and single digging. There are also a couple of tackle and bait shops servicing Lough Swilly in the Letterkenny and Buncrana regions.

Lough Swilly is probably most noted for tope fishing; the Rathmullan International Tope Angling Festival takes place in early June each year. The angling guide NRFB (2007) describes tope as a medium-sized shallow water shark, that can be found in the Swilly from late May/early June to September. They can reach up to 36kg in weight but catches tend to be around 18kg. A catch, weigh and release methodology is now used to conserve stocks of tope.

Mackerel is used as bait when fishing for tope, but a rubby dubby bag consisting of fish oils, entrails and bran contained in an onion bag, is placed over the side of the boat so that it just touches the water, leaving a trail behind it to attract the tope. To anglers feeling slightly sea sick the rubby dubby bag might just tip them over the edge!

The lough is also host to excellent ray fishing, in particular the homelyn (spotted ray) and the thornback ray, reaching 2kg and 5kg in weight, respectively.

The Inland Fisheries Ireland (formerly the Northern Regional Fisheries Board) has an excellent publication, *A guide to sea angling in the Donegal region,* that is well worth purchasing if considering sea angling in Lough Swilly. Experienced guides/guillies are also available to assist novices and to develop more advanced angling skills.

Charter boats run from Rathmullan (*Enterprise 1* and *Swilly Explorer*) and Portsalon (*The Meabh*) piers from May to September, but can also be hired outside these peak times. Species caught, usually at depths of 20–40m, include cod,

Table 10.2: Angling sites around Lough Swilly	
Location	*General information & species*
Dunaff Head	Rock perches south side of Head: ballan, corkwing wrasse with pollack and mackerel at high tides. Conger possible.
Leannan Head	North shore: pollack and mackerel in summer. Wrasse and coalfish; wider range of species from pier and rocks to the south: coalfish, wrasse, pollack and launce; casting over sand: ray, dogfish, codling, plaice and dab.
Dunree Head	Numerous suitable sites: wrasse, pollack, coalfish, dogfish, sometimes conger.
Stragill Beach	Trench-dinner for lugworm.
Buncrana	Float fishing: mackerel; sandy ground: ray, dogfish, whiting and dabs, sometimes sea trout (freshwater runoff effects catch).
Fahan	Best when tide incoming after dry spell: ray, dogfish and flounder.
Rathmullan pier	Best at night on slack tide: ray, tope on occasion but difficult to land; charter boats launch from pier.
Portsalon	Spinning: mackerel; bottom fishing: dabs, plaice, flounder, dogfish, sometimes ray; tidal site; best at night.
Fanad Head	Finger rock north of lighthouse in summer: pollack, coalfish, mackerel; occasional sea trout from rocks to the south; close to rocks: wrasse, coalfish; Pincer Bay: dabs, codling and ray; area also popular with birdwatchers.
wrecks	Gurnard family found in the outer area between Dunaff Head and Fanad Head; *Laurentic* wreck lies in 40m of water 4km off Fanad Head: ling, conger, pollack, coalfish, pouting and wrasse; *Audacious*, 32km from Portsalon.

10.5 A happy sea angler with a tope caught on the boat *Fisher Boy*, 1990. Photo: John Niven.

haddock, whiting, wrasse, dab and dogfish. These vessels are fully licensed and equipped for sea angling, and have diversified to cater for wildlife and sightseeing tours. Sea angling provides the opportunity to encounter dolphins, whales, basking sharks and a wide variety of sea birds.

GAME ANGLING ON LOUGH SWILLY

Three main salmonid rivers flow into Lough Swilly; two of these, though – the Leannan and the Swilly – have been unable to reach their conservation limits in recent years and have been closed. The conservation limit is calculated as the number of spawning fish required to maintain a self-sustaining population. Local angling clubs in association with the Inland Fisheries have started remedial work, which should result in increased salmonid runs. The Inland Fisheries (2010) has already seen an increase in redd (salmon 'nest') counts, which is promising for the future.

The Crana River remains open; this is a 12km-long spate river that flows into Lough Swilly north of Buncrana. It is managed by the Buncrana Angling Association and licences, permits and fishing tackle can be purchased from the Crana Angling Centre. A permit alone is not sufficient to fish for salmon and sea trout. A State licence is also required. There is a limit of 10 tags per angler per year. The salmon and sea trout season generally runs from 1 January to the 30 September with some exceptions, so it is best to check with a local angling club or the Inland Fisheries website (www.fishinginireland.info). All anglers are legally required to tag and record all salmon and any sea trout over 40cm in length. On-the-spot fines are issued to anglers who are found with untagged fish or fail to produce a logbook or licence.

10.6 Whale watching day at Dunree Fort. Photo: Emmett Johnston.

Game and sea angling in Donegal is marketed and sold via www.donegal anglingholidays.com. This site, run by Inland Fisheries Ireland, gives details of sustainably managed State-owned game angling rivers and sells rods online. It also provides direct links to sea angling providers. Special offers are available on the site where sea angling vessels have teamed up with local accommodation providers to improve the visitor experience. Lough Swilly features strongly in the sea angling section of the website.

Sailing and Boating in Lough Swilly

Sailing and boating in Lough Swilly is long established. The 1830s Ordnance Survey memoirs describe the Rathmullan regatta and detail the number of boats in parishes around the lough. Rathmullan is believed to be one of, if not the oldest, regattas in Ireland. Nowadays regattas are held in Fahan and Rathmullan over the August bank holiday weekend. The Rathmullan and Buncrana communities host festivals and activities around the regattas, including live open air music, poetry, sand castle building competitions, raft races and fancy dress. The Rathmullan Community Festival starts the week before the regatta with a hectic itinerary.

Lough Swilly Yacht Club runs the regattas. The club was founded in 1955 at the old railway station waiting room and ticket office. The first race took place on 2 July 1955. The club is based in Fahan, three miles south of Buncrana, and is thriving with over 250 members. It has a wide-ranging membership of IRC-racing and cruising sailors as well as power-boaters, and dinghy sailors.[1] The club

1 IRC is a means of rating different types of yacht, rather like a 'handicap' in golf.

10.7a Fahan marina viewed from the air. Photo: Emmett Johnston.

10.7b Rathmullan pontoon. Photo: Andrew Cooper.

organizes, and participates in, a wide range of races in addition to regattas. Races include the Limeburner race, a race to Tory and a race around Inch Island. Some members go much further afield to Iceland, the Canaries and France. The club also intends to offer sailing tuition in 2010.

Fahan marina provides berthing for the many club members as well as other resident and visiting boats. According to the club the marina facility has extended the sailing season over winter. Fahan marina has over 200 berths with plans to develop more.

10.8 Lough Swilly
Yacht Club event.
Photo: Lough Swilly
Yacht Club.

10.9 Rathmullan
Pico rigging small by
Rathmullan Sailing
School. Photo:
Rathmullan Sailing and
Watersports School.

Rathmullan Sailing and Water Sports School was established in 2008 and has already blossomed into a sailing club. It has strong links with Lough Swilly Yacht Club, which provided a safety vessel for the Rathmullan club in their first year. ISA-certified instructors offer three levels of courses: *A taste of sailing*, *Start sailing* and *Basic skills*. The courses are designed to get people with little or no experience on the water and provide them with the opportunity to improve to a stage where they can sail unaccompanied in light conditions. Courses range from 3 hours to 5 days. The club has a fleet of new Laser Pico dinghies and have plans for expansion in 2010. Courses are run primarily in summer but January 2010 saw their first 'Frostbite Regatta', which was a great success, and is an example of how there is opportunity to extend the water sports season. The school has provided a much-needed boost to the Rathmullan area as boating attracts onlookers and brings people to the village for extended periods. It has also reawakened an interest in the fun and economic potential Lough Swilly has to offer.

Atlantic Navigation based in Milford provides ISA-approved level 1, 2 and Advanced power-boating courses. They operate from Rathmullan pier and have growing links with the water sports school and club.

Buncrana harbour is home to the Lough Swilly Sea Safari (www.loughswilly seasafari.com), which departs every hour on Saturdays and Sundays from May to August. The boat can take twelve passengers and it is a great way to experience Lough Swilly. Sightings of basking sharks, dolphins, seals and birdlife are all possible. The sea safari is catered to the tastes of its passengers ranging from history buffs to out-and-out thrill seekers.

Development, Economic Potential and Management

Practically all of the activities and the majority of commercial activities that take place in the area rely on the natural resources Lough Swilly provides. Sustainable use of this resource is required to ensure that it still exists for future generations. The loss of some habitats may not seem important in the grand scale of things and may not seem apparent at first, but the impact of losing one link in the biodiversity chain can have quite devastating effects on an area.

In addition to sustainable environmental management, visitors and residents using Lough Swilly may want, and expect, to get different things from the Swilly. Many visitors come to its shores for peace and tranquillity, while others come for the adrenalin and thrill a fast powerboat trip can give. Accommodating these competing demands provides a challenge. A 2008 report by Royal Haskoning identified quality themes for the Rathmullan area that are transferable to all areas around the Swilly. These include landscape (in relation to marine tourism activities); the environment and the potential this holds for future recreation and leisure activity; quality of life in the community, including factors such as the rural character; the hospitality of the local people and the quality of food service within the region.

The Potential of Marine Tourism and Leisure

Several EU directives are relevant to the marine and coastal environment and its industries. They seek to promote sustainable employment, integrated development, tourism, marine spatial planning and climate change. These policies and directives provide the platform for Irish legislation, policy and strategic development. A 2007 Marine Institute report found that marine/coastal tourism and leisure in Ireland had no strategic leadership or coherent policy, and that for it to contribute fully to the country's socio-economic development these issues need to be addressed. The Institute estimates the national revenue generated by the tourism and leisure sector at €631m, based on the value of domestic business, overseas tourism and associated retail services. It has the potential to grow to c.€1billion by 2013.

The Marine Institute concluded that water-based activities could make a very significant contribution to domestic tourism in Ireland, not by attracting a huge specialist domestic market per se, but by contributing to the overall experience of many domestic tourists. The Institute states that water-based tourism can make a

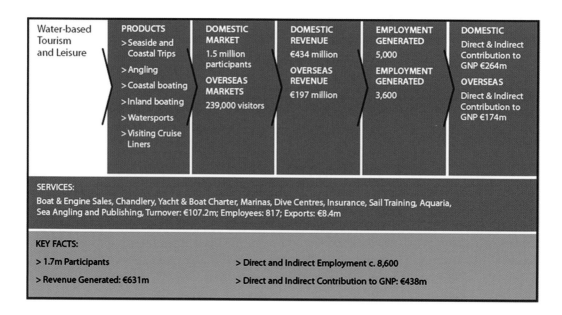

| Water-based Tourism and Leisure | PRODUCTS > Seaside and Coastal Trips > Angling > Coastal boating > Inland boating > Watersports > Visiting Cruise Liners | DOMESTIC MARKET 1.5 million participants OVERSEAS MARKETS 239,000 visitors | DOMESTIC REVENUE €434 million OVERSEAS REVENUE €197 million | EMPLOYMENT GENERATED 5,000 EMPLOYMENT GENERATED 3,600 | DOMESTIC Direct & Indirect Contribution to GNP €264m OVERSEAS Direct & Indirect Contribution to GNP €174m |

SERVICES:
Boat & Engine Sales, Chandlery, Yacht & Boat Charter, Marinas, Dive Centres, Insurance, Sail Training, Aquaria, Sea Angling and Publishing, Turnover: €107.2m; Employees: 817; Exports: €8.4m

KEY FACTS:

> 1.7m Participants   > Direct and Indirect Employment c. 8,600

> Revenue Generated: €631m   > Direct and Indirect Contribution to GNP: €438m

Economic importance of Irish water-based tourism and leisure. From Marine Institute, 2007.

more significant contribution at a regional level to economic sustainability and environmental objectives. Though no specific study has been carried out on the economic value of marine tourism and leisure to Donegal, from the information available from the Marine Institute, Donegal County Council and Inland Fisheries Ireland, it is estimated that the direct and indirect value to the Donegal economy is between €25m and €35m annually. A 2006 Marine Institute report contends that

> A proliferation of natural resources is not sufficient in itself. Counties with strong tourism industries that are customer focussed will fare best in promoting marine tourism.

The Water-based Tourism and Leisure Product Audit 2006 identified that the marine leisure product in County Donegal had gaps in sailing, boating, water sports facilities and marine/water-themed visitor centres. Services were found to be lacking on beaches and all products require improvement and development of promotion, packaging, service links and organization. Sea angling was categorized as an excellent product that can be brought to the market immediately, but again requires packaging, promotion and service links.

Lough Swilly is well placed to benefit from local, national and European policies, strategies and assessments. Tourism in the Swilly region is already focused on a number of these product areas, and it has the potential to fill some of the product gaps identified by the Marine Institute.

The Future

Many marine tourism providers also have jobs in other fields; this is partly because tourism in the area is so seasonal and because some businesses have evolved from

10.10 Lough Swilly Yacht Club – dingy sailing. Photo: Lough Swilly Yacht Club.

10.11 Traditional sailing boats mingle with bathers on the beach at Rathmullan. Photo: Andrew Cooper.

a hobby. It is therefore often the 'second earner' and perhaps as a consequence isn't exploited to its full potential. The Marine Institute (2007) states that there is a need to build a market presence on the internet and to ensure that water-based holidays are branded and integrated with other tourism services. It cites the north-west as a serious underperformer, saying that Donegal, in particular, has the resources and accommodation base to benefit quickly from a greater concentration in marine tourism.

A 2009 report by Kevin Bonner suggests that Donegal could take a lead from the marine tourism market in the south-west. He concludes that Donegal can compete successfully in the specialist overseas markets for angling, boating, sailing and water sports. He also states that game angling, sea angling, beach holidays and water sports are reasonably well organized in the county, and there is an interest from both public and private investors in relation to marinas, sailing and boating. Lough Swilly is well endowed with all of these products and resources.

With regard to branding, Donegal has a name for surfing and a good reputation for clean beaches and angling. Game angling on state rivers and sea angling is now organized and ready for the international market. An online sales mechanism has been established for these products (www.donegalanglingholidays.com).

The Marine leisure and tourism industry on Lough Swilly is diverse and scattered. It is clearly evolving as different opportunities arise and business ventures respond. It too, like other activities, has to try and co-exist with other demands, some of which are competitive while others are complementary.

Chapter 11

Managing Lough Swilly

Andrew Cooper and Marianne O'Connor

Introduction

As we have seen throughout this book, Lough Swilly is a living and changing environment. Since its initial sculpting during the ice ages, it has seen major ups and downs of sea level, been exposed to centuries of waves and tides and hundreds of storms, been colonized by a diverse plant and animal life and has been exploited by people since the first settlers set foot in Ireland. From then on it has provided a valuable resource for people living around its shores and far beyond. Its importance to people has changed with time, but through the changing centuries of history, the lough has continued its ebb and flow, sustaining life and providing a backdrop to a diversity of human activities.

The contemporary landscape is a mosaic that blends the imprints of bygone times with those of modern activities; no doubt the lough and its surroundings will continue to change into the future. Throughout the centuries of human utilization of Lough Swilly people have adapted to the changing natural environment and changes in the wider world. Activities have come and gone as resources were depleted, new resources were identified, markets and fashions changed, technology improved, and generations arrived and departed.

Over the years, various forms of regulation with penalties and incentives have been used to curtail or encourage human activities; for example, subsidies were paid to encourage fisheries in the eighteenth century, grants were made available to encourage development of landing places in the nineteenth century and gaps were installed in salmon weirs following legislation in 1866. At present activities on and around the lough are affected by a host of government departments implementing and enforcing local, national and international policies and laws. To date, the degree of integration between these bodies has been somewhat lacking and many go about their own business without a great deal of reference to other players.

In the past twenty years, a number of attempts have been made by the European Commission to achieve integration in the management of different sectors of human activity. There have been experiments in integrated coastal zone management (ICZM) across Europe and ongoing initiatives to manage the coast and adjacent waters by directives aimed at the introduction of marine spatial planning (MSP). Two beaches on the Swilly (Lisfannon and Portsalon) featured in a pilot project by the University of Ulster and Donegal County Council in the

EU's 'Demonstration Programme in ICZM' from 1996 to 1999. Recently, the EU's Water Framework Directive has established a framework for managing water from the river catchment through to the nearshore coastal zones. These initiatives are based on the recognition that coastal resources throughout Europe have been seriously degraded by human activities and that halting and reversing this trend will require an integrated approach – much more easily said than done. To date, it is common for activities above the high water line to be managed quite separately from those below it. It is also common practice for different activities to be managed quite independently of each other by different government departments, or even different parts of the same government department. In this chapter, some of the management issues in Lough Swilly are discussed in relation to the need for a better, integrated system for managing diverse activities in the face of environmental change.

Regulation of various activities has been practised in Ireland for centuries, usually to protect the interest of that particular activity rather than in an integrated way. The pressures from modern forms of mainly mechanized exploitation, coupled with greater accessibility due to modern transport, mean that threats to the lough are now much greater than in the past. In addition, there are now many instances where different activities are in competition for the same resource and without integrated management, conflicts will arise.

The prospect of rapid global climate change also gives cause for much concern for human activities on, and around, the lough. Some aspects of the lough's ecosystem like shellfish growth rates or bird migration routes may be affected directly, while human activities (for example, shellfishing, recreation and farming) may experience indirect effects.

Adaptation to changed circumstances involves a change in human activities and expectations. The people of the Swilly region have clearly adapted in the past to changing political, environmental and economic circumstances. When climate change caused the collapse of the herring fishery, new fisheries were exploited. When the agricultural economy came under the remit of the Common Agricultural Policy, farming practice responded. While the property boom ran, there was a dramatic increase in the rate and extent of construction and when it stopped, development stopped equally abruptly. All of these examples show to a greater or lesser extent that humans are adaptable to external and internal forces. Modern thinking maintains that our adaptation, however, should run more smoothly when it is planned.

With all of this in mind, this chapter looks at some of the issues that arise from conflicts between different lough users. It goes on to consider future climate change and some of its potential influences on the lough.

Global and Local Climate Change

Meteorologists and other scientists have assembled evidence of a gradual warming of the earth's air temperatures, a melting of ice caps and a rise in global sea level.

This is attributed to increases in greenhouse gases in the atmosphere, which in turn is the result of industrial development and very rapid population growth. In fact geologists have recognized this as an entirely new geological epoch, which they have called the 'Anthropocene', meaning that humans are the dominant global geological force. While these changes are happening at a global scale they will have implications for Lough Swilly and its surroundings. It is impossible to predict with accuracy what the future holds but there are some general trends that provide an indication. The temperatures will increase and the sea level will begin to rise. The models used to predict climate change into the future suggest that winters will become wetter and summers dryer and there may be more intense rainfall events leading to more frequent river floods.

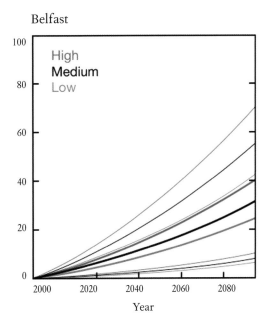

11.1 Relative sea level (RSL) rise in cm over the twenty-first century showing central estimate values (thick lines) and 5th and 95th percentile limits of the range of uncertainty (thin lines) for Belfast. Values are relative to 1990. Belfast occupies a similar position to much of Lough Swilly in relation to land uplift rates and so the rates are likely to be directly applicable.

A 2009 report by Fáilte Ireland explored the implications of climate change for Ireland's natural and built heritage. These include:

- the coastal landscape may suffer due to increased frequency and intensity in the storm and water surges and coastal erosion;
- changes in air/water temperature and precipitation may cause Ireland's landscape to change, and may exacerbate existing pollution problems. This would put greater pressure on species of invertebrates, fish and plants and ultimately tourism industries such as sea angling;
- rising sea levels may make Ireland less suitable for existing species of plants and animals, causing them to become stressed or even extinct. Sandwich terns are believed to be at particular risk on Inch Lake.

Mean sea level around the Swilly has been stable for the past century and probably for several hundred years since global sea level rise has been equalled by land uplift in north Donegal. In the future this is likely to change as accelerated global sea level rise gets the upper hand over land uplift. To what degree sea level will rise, and over what timescale, is difficult to tell.

According to the UK Climate Impacts Programme (UKCIP 09) data, increases in relative sea levels are likely to continue and accelerate but the extent of these are uncertain and dependent on emissions trends. Figure 11.1 illustrates the range uncertainty in these increases. Work undertaken for the National Trust in Northern Ireland suggests sea level could rise by as much as 1m in the next 100 years.

Rainfall patterns are also anticipated to change with winter rainfall in Ireland projected to increase by 10% and summer rainfall to reduce by 12–14% by 2050.

11.2 Protection of the golf course at Lisfannon by rock armour has preserved the course, but the beach has narrowed and sediment supply to the beaches at Fahan has been reduced. Photo: Nigel McDowell.

Trends in sea and air temperature also predict a rise with temperatures currently increasing at 0.2–0.6°C per decade. The last decade has produced seven of the ten warmest years on record. These increases in sea temperatures are also increasing ocean acidification. So how will these changes affect Lough Swilly?

Increases in sea level and precipitation would be expected to result in an increased risk of flooding, coastal erosion, breaching of coastal defences, instability of exposed slopes, changes in water quality and loss of habitats and amenity around the lough. Low lying areas of land such as Letterkenny and the reclaimed agricultural land around Inch Levels would be vulnerable to loss from sea-level rise. There are a number of ways in which these areas can be managed depending on the type of land and the level of economic dependency of the area.

Flood and erosion risk may be tackled in four main ways:

1. protection – build new or improve existing defences.
2. accommodating – allows continued occupancy of vulnerable areas through adaptation to, rather than protection from, adverse impacts.
3. managed retreat – allow low-lying land to be inundated. Involves relocation of coastal communities and a prohibition on further development.
4. do nothing – no action is taken at all; this is only viable when the coastline is undeveloped.

Coastal defences operate by reducing the possibility of flooding or erosion. They require periodic maintenance, which have associated costs. They are likely to interact with the prevailing coastal processes and have the potential to alter the morphology not only in the immediate area, but also further afield. Their presence can stop the development and movement of natural habitats and result in the loss

of habitat such as coastal wetlands due to 'coastal squeeze'. It is therefore the case that options 2, 3 and 4 are more sustainable from a geomorphological point of view, although not necessarily from a socio-economic perspective.

Increases in rainfall may impact on agricultural practice, and as this would result in changes in runoff patterns it could have an effect on water quality. Influxes of excess nutrients, coupled with increases in sea and air temperature, may result in harmful algal blooms. It is also possible that the reduction in rainfall predicted for summer months may decrease nutrient input.

Changes in air temperature may result in changes in tourism patterns with an increase in tourist numbers and recreational use of the lough due to an extended tourist season. This type of opportunity could be at risk if water quality is not managed correctly.

Increases in water temperature also pose a risk to the fishing and aquaculture sector. The fishing industry is vulnerable to the predicted effects of climate change because seasonal cycles of fish reproduction are temperature dependent and sensitive to small changes in temperature over relatively short time scales. This could result in changes in the growth rate of commercial species and a rise in occurrence of warm water species. Changes in sea temperature may also increase the risk of diseases being introduced; however, it could also result in faster growth rates or the potential to grow new species. Ocean acidification can affect shellfish development as acidic conditions are not conducive to shell formation. The

11.3 Erosion of the beach at Lisfannon. The beach which had developed through accumulation of sand from the north has now been starved of fresh sand by the seawall at the golf club. Vain efforts to slow the erosion have been attempted using soft engineering. Photo: Nigel McDowell.

11.4 Protection of a caravan site and apartments on Fahan Creek by rock armour and seawalls. This highlights the link between development at the coast and impacts on the environment. Without such developments, coastal erosion would not have been an issue. Building close to the coast creates an erosion problem. Photo: Andrew Cooper.

inundation of freshwater areas with salt water may impact on spawning areas – impacting the habitat structure of the area and also affecting the angling community.

Acidification can also affect the stability of concrete structures. The occurrence of more severe winter weather conditions, even if they occur less frequently than at present, would have an impact upon fishing vessels and ferry timetables and put pressure on berthing structures.

The predicted climate changes described above are uncertain; it is clear though, that even if current trends continue, the Lough Swilly environment and community will be affected by coastal change.

Resource Conflicts

Not every activity on Lough Swilly meets with universal approval. This is not uncommon when different activities compete for the same space or resource, or when various groups of people appreciate or derive benefits from different values of the resource. Some visitors come to Lough Swilly for peace and tranquillity, while others come for the adrenalin and thrill of a fast powerboat trip. Accommodating these competing demands provides a challenge.

This kind of situation is widespread in waters around the world and it is particularly acute in situations where different government bodies are responsible for different activities. Typically, each of those government bodies promotes and defends the interests of its clients and there is often no mechanism to resolve the issues by bringing the warring sides together. In the absence of an integrated

11.5 Formerly reclaimed land north of Ramelton. The defensive wall has been broken during storms and has not been replaced. The sea is now flooding into the area, turning it back to mudflats and salt marsh. This type of retreat in the face of coastal erosion and sea level rise is becoming more common in Europe as agricultural land has a lower premium than in the period when it was reclaimed. Photo: Marianne O'Connor.

approach to management through ICZM or MSP, conflicts continue to play out in the press and at public meetings as the warring factions press forward their cases to their respective representatives. For example, in the absence of an integrated approach to licensing of marine activities, a petition was launched on 13 January 2001 by the Save the Swilly Group, demanding a moratorium on all further aquaculture licensing in Lough Swilly until an independent study of the issue was undertaken. Submitted to the European Parliament in 2002, it elicited several replies from the European Commission up to April 2010, in which the Commission criticized aspects of Lough Swilly's management and advocated an integrated approach.

Without an integrated approach to management, we cannot tell whether the lough is being put to the most effective, or the most acceptable, use. It is also impossible without integration to balance local and national short- and long-term perspectives. This conflict is personified by the different views of aquaculture on Lough Swilly. Strong arguments have been made for and against the extent and type of aquaculture being practised. These are outlined in geographyinaction.co.uk and are further elaborated below.

Arguments for Aquaculture

ECONOMY

Proponents of aquaculture argue that it is an important economic activity, particularly in rural and peripheral areas where jobs are greatly needed. They contend that the activity is widespread in rural areas and is generally accepted by local people. Geographyinaction.co.uk reports that 'one study found a very positive attitude to aquaculture by local people due to the long term, high quality employment it provides'. It has also been argued that every €1 of public money

11.6 Aquaculture has been a controversial activity in the Swilly. There is currently no means of weighing up its pros and cons and testing its acceptability in comparison to other competing uses. To some it may, like windmills, simply reflect a new phase in the ever-changing cultural imprint, while to others it is a blot on the landscape, incompatible with other uses. Photo: Nigel McDowell.

invested in aquaculture produces earnings of €2.85 each year. There are an estimated 2,200 people working on fish farms in Ireland on a full- and part-time basis, and others are employed in producing foodstuffs and materials and in processing and marketing the produce. It has further been claimed that every person involved in salmon farming, for example, generates a further 1.26 jobs. Advocates of aquaculture claim that the output and economic benefit from aquaculture will increase in the future and new species are being developed and farmed. The importance of the industry is evidenced in its inclusion in the National Development Plan (2000–6). The National Development Plan (2007–13) notes its economic importance and states that 'it will therefore be necessary during the plan period to develop other industries such as aquaculture, tourism and the leisure industry to provide alternate means of employment'. Interestingly, the plan envisages 'the emergence of a smaller number of larger operators in this sector, working on greater economies of scale'.

ENVIRONMENT

Proponents argue that the presence of aquaculture in an area has many positive environmental impacts; for example, aquaculture species, particularly shellfish, provide an additional food source for birds in the culture area. There are stringent EU regulations regarding sewage pollution near aquaculture sites and a classification of shellfish waters is in place throughout Europe. Thus aquaculture provides an additional economic motivation for maintaining good water quality and places greater pressure on government to improve sewage treatment facilities in rural areas. Lough Swilly was downgraded by the European Union from A to B status in August 2001. After that, shellfish could be used for human consumption only after treatment in a purification plant.

A spokesman for BIM (Bord Iascaigh Mhara – the Irish Sea Fisheries Board), was quoted by geographyinaction.co.uk as saying 'The fact is, it will be left up to fish farmers, as the only group who actively makes their living from the bay, to highlight and fight this serious threat to the environment [poor water quality]'. The Irish Shellfish Association is therefore encouraging the government to improve sewage treatment facilities in the hope of Lough Swilly's water quality being improved and supporters argue that if there were no active shellfish industry, this campaign would not be taking place.

The BIM spokesman also stated that aquaculture is 'virtually an invisible process with no possible visual or environmental impacts whatsoever.' He added that only a small proportion of the lough would be used for aquaculture. 'Lough Swilly has a total area of 16,600 hectares. If you combine all the areas that are under application for intensive aquaculture, either shellfish or salmon farming, the total area would be no more than 160 hectares. That's marginally less than 1% of the total area of the lough.'

MANAGEMENT

This Co-ordinated Local Aquaculture Management System (CLAMS) for Lough Swilly produces Codes of Practice for the cultivation of the different species and a framework for addressing and resolving issues arising from aquaculture. It also provides information on other activities in Lough Swilly such as marine tourism, bird watching and wildlife that can be of use to other sectors. In the absence of a co-ordinated approach to management of the lough, this is a valuable information resource.

TOURISM AND AQUACULTURE

A spokesman for the Irish Salmon Growers Association argues that fish farming attracts visitors to an area as 'visitors prefer to see activity and people using resources rather than "dead bays".' Elsewhere in the world, some tourism has been organized around aquaculture activity, with guided tours to production sites and interpretation centres. Such developments require careful management and planning if they are to minimize interference with aquaculture activities and provide a good tourism experience.

Arguments against Aquaculture

Opponents to aquaculture in Lough Swilly fear that the government has decided to designate Lough Swilly primarily for aquaculture and that considerable expansion is planned. An umbrella organisation comprising a variety of interest groups and residents opposed to aquaculture is known as Save the Swilly. Its spokesman, Mr John Mulcahy, voiced its concerns over 'the failure of the regulatory authorities to adopt an objective stance towards the sector. The Irish government has taken a stand in favour of aquaculture rather than as an objective arbitrator in the process. Consequently, it behaves as an advocate of the industry, and justifies its decisions to licence large tracts of public waters for the aquaculture industry without adequate analysis of the risks'.

WATER QUALITY

Opponents to fish farming argue that up to 19 different chemicals are regularly required and legally approved in the production of farmed salmon, for example. These range from pesticides to control the growth of pests that can proliferate in the salmon cages, anti-fouling paints to prevent the growth of seaweeds on the cages and nets, and antibiotics to control disease. These chemicals, along with faeces and excess food, can pollute the water or gather as sediment on the seabed.

ECONOMICS

Opponents estimate that Lough Swilly aquaculture employs no more than 20 people. It is claimed that 600 people are employed in hotels, guesthouses and B&Bs and many more people in Inishowen and in Fanad depend on tourism, directly and indirectly. If, as a result of aquaculture development, Lough Swilly loses the qualities of unspoilt beauty, scenic routes, wild fish angling, clean seawater and safe beaches that make the area attractive to tourists then jobs will be threatened. Save the Swilly claims that 'Tourism providers relate frequent complaints about the sight – and smell – of nearby fish cages'.

Opponents question the economics of shellfish aquaculture in Ireland, contending that the value of shellfish such as mussels and oysters sold in markets in Europe is mostly retained by wholesalers and other intermediaries outside Ireland. Save the Swilly claims that 'The proportion of the final selling price of mussels and oysters that is retained in Ireland is no more than 25% in most cases, suggesting that Ireland is purely a commodity producer, and most of the margin in the business is in the hands of traders. There is a need for a comprehensive review of the industry, taking account of environmental aspects and also the value chain, and why most of the value is conceded to offshore operators'.

CONSERVATION

There is concern worldwide about the decline in wild salmon stocks and many people point at fish farming as the cause of such decline. There is suspicion that sea lice which commonly infest farmed salmon can transfer themselves to wild salmon and lead to a spread in diseases. Escapes of salmon have occurred elsewhere in Ireland and those opposed to fish farming argue that their interbreeding with wild stocks could be very damaging. Similar concerns have been voiced about native shellfish and the introduction of disease via farmed stock. *Crassostrea gigas* oysters have been recognized in Northern Ireland (Strangford lough) as an alien invasive species, and in Lough Swilly there is concern over their encroachment into native oyster habitats.

Save the Swilly argues 'the government is evidently sympathetic to the impact sea-lice has on salmon farms, but appears to have little regard for the impact of sea-lice to the surrounding environment. Concerns about the impact of sea-lice from salmon farms on salmon rivers, on sea trout and on the migratory routes for salmon have not been addressed and regulators dismiss such concerns with the response that there is no evidence of a causal link between the decline of sea trout and wild salmon stocks and sea-lice from salmon farms.'

The EC Directorate-General for the Environment has conveyed its concerns about aquaculture expansion in Lough Swilly's Special Protection Areas to the Irish government. There is also concern that habitats for migrating and native wildfowl are under threat. Local people believe they are not properly consulted when licenses are granted for aquaculture and that their objections are therefore being ignored.

NAVIGATION

The development of aquaculture sites means that those areas are no longer available for other users as the aquaculture equipment prevents both fishing and pleasure boats from using the area. More than 80 people are permanently employed in commercial fishing around Lough Swilly, with another 200 seasonal jobs. As their craft are not sufficiently large to brave the Atlantic storms in winter, the loss to fishing of areas of the lough could have a significant impact on these fishermen.

BAD MANAGEMENT

Opponents see aquaculture being vigorously supported at the expense of other activities and bemoan the lack of integrated management. They maintain that government has not met its commitment to Integrated Coastal Zone Management (ICZM), implicit in the Water Framework Directive, and in a 2002 EU Recommendation. Save the Swilly maintains that ICZM 'has been systematically rejected or ignored'. They argue that 'It is sound practice to assess the impact of a new activity on the basis of evidence before proceeding, and in the context of aquaculture licensing this means analyzing the carrying capacity of the bays in which aquaculture is proposed. Simply stating that the surface area of Lough Swilly is 16,000 hectares and aquaculture occupies only a fraction of that is not science. The location of aquaculture within the bay needs to be assessed, along with the probable impact on other activities or indeed on the preferences of the community most affected by the process. Overall, the inherent conflict of interest within the Irish system, whereby the same Government department is responsible for licensing, regulation and promotion of aquaculture, means that there is little or

11.7 Residential housing has spread along the shores of the lough, particularly during the housing boom of the 2000s. While it brought economic prosperity for a time, the boom has turned to bust. Development like this falls under existing planning control, but there are additional impacts on waste disposal and water quality, visual quality, transport and infrastructure and additional pressures on the lough. Bringing the waters of the lough into the same type of regulatory environment (called Marine Spatial Planning) could help resolve issues and plan the use of the lough more efficiently. Photo: Marianne O'Connor.

no incentive to (a) regulate the industry effectively, or (b) to enforce licence conditions'.

Integrated Management of Lough Swilly

The ongoing debate around aquaculture is simply indicative of issues that commonly arise in coastal management. The debate summarized above highlights the competing demands for coastal resources and demonstrates the diversity of views that can exist. It is impossible to resolve such issues without taking an integrated approach to coastal management. Even then there can be winners and losers, but a properly integrated system allows for all issues to be discussed together and allows for informed management decisions to be made.

> Just think for a moment of how much an integrated approach can boost the prosperity of coastal regions, while assuring environmental protection of the seas and thus allowing for the continued development of tourism. Just think how an integrated approach could help ease the consequences of climate change, like rising sea levels and increased virulence and frequency of storms, by supporting continued investment in economic activity in coastal regions. A coordinated approach, including increased use of structural funds, will have to ensure that global warming does not become an impediment to growth and job creation in coastal regions.
>
> *José Manuel Barossa, President of the European Commission*

11.8 Economic development is much needed in Donegal and the Fruit of the Loom factory in Buncrana provided much-needed jobs for a time. Now that the factory has closed it has become, like the warehouses at Ramelton, a visible reminder of another age. Photo: Andrew Cooper.

Lough Swilly is a finite resource; finding a balance between making a living, protecting the resource and having fun is a challenge that requires an integrated or 'joined-up' approach. Without it, conflicts abound and sub-optimal use is made of the resource. The issues are the same for existing conflicts and for coping with the impacts of climate change. At present numerous state agencies and Donegal County Council are involved in the management of Lough Swilly and the activities that take place in, on and around it. Similar issues are faced in many coastal zones and the sustainable and integrated development of the coast, both land and water, is an issue at European, national and local level.

Local Authorities have a statutory role in planning and integrated local development, and are therefore important players in the development of the marine and coastal resource. The Donegal County Development Plan (CDP) 2006–12 describes the region surrounding Lough Swilly as an area of High Scenic Amenity and identifies tourism products that should provide a focus for future development. These include marine leisure, walking, angling, flagship projects, festivals and cultural events, heritage / culture and tourist routes. The CDP also has policies for integrated coastal zone management, and the development of a centre for coastal zone education and research in the county. National government departments, rather than local authorities, have responsibility for many activities on Lough Swilly and sustainable management requires some way of integrating their management actions with each other as well as with the local authorities.

Some issues that affect Lough Swilly transcend the local context and require action at higher levels. Debates, for example, about the ethics, sustainability and desirability of marine aquaculture, or of the need to mitigate climate change by reducing CO_2 emissions are high-level debates that demand national and international attention. Other issues such as what activities are conducted where, and at what times, are clearly of local interest and the views of competing and

11.9 Holiday home development was one of the most dramatic effects of the property boom. Generally having low occupancy rates and having questionable long-term economic benefit to the region, these types of development become part of the landscape whether occupied or not. Photo: Andrew Cooper.

complementary activities deserve to be heard in the decision-making process. This concept is central to the notion of integrated coastal zone management (ICZM). A variety of mechanisms for delivering ICZM has been tested to try to find an operational model. They range from voluntary partnerships to more formal systems involving spatial planning. Spatial planning is a tried and tested approach on land and is best seen locally in the County Development Plans that are intended to regulate land-use for the greater public benefit. Currently, there is much interest at European level in extending this approach into the sea, and developing systems for marine spatial planning (MSP).

Although ICZM and MSP have been in existence for some time, neither has been formally adopted in Ireland. The implementation of Marine Spatial Planning appears to be gaining momentum within the European Commission and it seems likely that some system will be applied in the future. MSP is in some ways similar to terrestrial planning by which we regulate the use of the land surface. It zones water areas for various uses and regulates those uses. It has an important difference to terrestrial planning in that it applies to the surface of the water, the water itself and the seabed. All of these have distinctive characteristics and uses and all of them are continually changing, which makes MSP more complex than terrestrial planning.

Whatever initiatives eventually arise, it is clear that Lough Swilly faces such a diverse range of pressures and conflicts, high demand from a growing population, and such threats from global climate change that an integrated management approach is urgently needed. With this approach we might be able to achieve sustainable development (meeting the needs of the present generation without compromising the ability of future generations to meet their own needs). Without it, future generations might inherit a landscape of conflict and degeneration.

Further Reading

Bass, N. 2002. Sources, production and fate of nutrients in Lough Swilly and its catchment. Report to the Lough Swilly. CLAMS group.

Beattie, S. 1999. William Hart of Muff and the Lough Swilly Oyster Company. *Donegal Annual*, 51, 62–70.

Benetti, S., Dunlop, P. and O'Cofaigh, C. 2010. Glacial and glacially-related features on the continental margin of northwest Ireland mapped from marine geophysical data. *Journal of Maps*, 5, 14–29.

Bord Iascaigh Mhara (BIM), 2001. Coordinated Local Area Management Scheme (CLAMS) Report Lough Swilly. BIM, Dublin.

Boelens, R., Minchin, D. & O'Sullivan, G. 2005. Climate change. Implications for Ireland's Marine Environment and Resources. Marine Foresight Series, 2. Marine Institute, Galway.

British Geological Survey (BGS) 1986. *Malin. Sheet 55N 08W Seabed Sediments and Quaternary*, Geological Map, Scale 1:250,000. Natural Environment Research Council, Edinburgh.

Campbell & Co. Design Consultants with Jura Consultants. 2007. Inch Levels Feasibility Study, Final report.

Clabby, K.J., Bradley, C., Craig, M., Daly, D., Lucey, J., McGarrigle, M., O'Boyle, S., Tierney, D. and Bowman, J. 2008. *Water Quality in Ireland, 2004–2006*. Environmental Protection Agency, Johnstown Castle, County Wexford.

Cooper, J.A.G., Kelley, J.T., Belknap, D.F., Quinn, R., McKenna, J. 2002. Inner shelf seismic stratigraphy off the north coast of Northern Ireland: new data on the depth of the Holocene lowstand. *Marine Geology*, 186, 369–87.

Cooper, J.A.G. and McKenna, J. 2008. Social Justice and coastal erosion management: the temporal and spatial dimensions. *Geoforum*, 39, 294–306.

Cooper, J.A.G. and McKenna, J. 2009. Boom and bust: the influence of macroscale economics on the world's coast. *Journal of Coastal Research*, 25, 533–8.

CSPI, 1601. '*The names of all the chief places of strength in O'Dogherty's country called Ennisowen, as well castles as forts; also of those in McSwyne Fanat's country*' (Calendar of State Papers, Ireland 1601, 276–9).

Day, A. & McWilliams, P. (editors) 1997. *Ordnance Survey memoirs, parishes of County Donegal 1, 1833–5*, North East Donegal, Vol. 38, Institute of Irish Studies, Queen's University, Belfast, 1997.

De Courcy Ireland, J. 1981. *Ireland's sea fisheries*, Glendale Press, Dublin.

Dunlop, Norman, 2007, *A guide to sea angling in the Donegal Region*. Northern Regional Fisheries Board.

Dunlop, P., Shannon, R., McCabe, M., Quinn, R., Doyle, E. 2010. Marine geophysical evidence for ice sheet extension and recession on the Malin Shelf: new evidence for the western limits of the British Irish Ice Sheet. *Marine Geology*, 276, 86–99.

Evans, D. 1973. A shallow seismic survey in Lough Swilly and Trawbreaga Bay, Co. Donegal. *Proceedings of the Royal Irish Academy*, 73B, 207–16.

EPA 2009. *Shellfish Pollution Reduction Program*. Characterisation Report Number 28, Lough Swilly Shellfish Area, County Donegal.

Hutton J.W. 1892, *Arthur Young's tour in Ireland* (1776–9), Vol. 1, George Bell and Sons, London.

Kelley, J.T., Cooper, J.A.G., Jackson, D.W.T., Belknap, D.F., Quinn, R.J. 2006. Sea-level change and inner shelf stratigraphy off Northern Ireland. *Marine Geology*, 232, 1–15.

Kerrigan P. 1995, *Castles and fortifications in Ireland*, Collins Press, Cork.

Kimbal, M. J. 2000, *Human ecology and Neolithic transition in Eastern County Donegal, Ireland: the Lough Swilly archaeological survey*, Oxford: British Archaeological Reports (British Series), 2000.

Lacy, B., 1983. *Archaeological survey of County Donegal*. Lifford.

Long, C.B., McConnell, B.J. 1997. Geology of North Donegal. *Geological survey of Ireland*, Dublin.

Mac Airt, S. and Mac Niocaill, G. (editor and translator) 1983. *The Annals of Ulster (to AD 1131), Part 1, Text and Translation*, Dublin Institute for Advanced Studies.

MacCarthaigh, C. (editor) 2008. *Traditional boats of Ireland*. Collins Press, Cork.

MacLeod, M., Pereira da Silva, C. & Cooper, J.A.G. 2002. A comparative study of the perception and value of beaches in rural Ireland and Portugal: implications for coastal zone management. *Journal of Coastal Research*, 18, 14–24.

Marine Institute, 2006. Water-based Tourism and Leisure Product Audit. Galway.

Marine Institute, 2007. National Strategy from development of Marine Tourism 2007–13. Galway.

McCabe, A.M. 1997. Geological constraints on geophysical models of relative sea level change during deglaciation of the western Irish Sea Basin. *Journal of the Geological Society of London*, 154, 601–4.

McCabe, A.M. 2008. *Glacial geology and geomorphology. The landscapes of Ireland*. Dunedin Press, Edinburgh.

McCabe, A.M and Dunlop, P. 2006. *The last glacial termination in Northern Ireland*. Geological Survey of Northern Ireland.

McElwain, L. and Sweeney, J. 2003. Climate change in Ireland. Recent trends in temperature and precipitation. *Irish Geography*, 36, 97–111.

McErlean, T. and O'Sullivan, A. 2002. Foreshore tidal fish traps. In: McErlean, T., McConkey, R. & Forsythe, W. *Strangford Lough. An archaeological survey of the maritime cultural landscape*, Northern Ireland Archaeological Monographs No. 6, Blackstaff Press, Belfast, 144–80.

McKenna, J., O'Hagan, A.M., Macleod, M.J., Power, J. & Cooper, J.A.G. 2003. Obsolete maps and coastal management: case studies from northwest Ireland. *Coastal Management*, 31, 229–46.

McKenna, J., Cooper, J.A.G. and O'Hagan, A.M. 2008. Managing by principle: a critical assessment of the EU principles of ICZM. *Marine Policy*, 32, 941–55.

McKenna, J., Power, J., Macleod, M. & Cooper, J.A.G. 2000. *Rural beach management: a good practice guide*. Donegal County Council, Lifford, Ireland.

McKenna, J. and Cooper, J.A.G. 2006. Sacred cows in coastal management: the need for a cheap and transitory model. *Area*, 38, 421–31.

Ní Loingsigh, M. 1997. An assessment of castles and landownership on Late Medieval North Donegal. *Ulster Journal of Archaeology* 57, 1994 (published 1997), 145–58.

Nolan, Pat. 2010. *Following the shoals*. The History Press Ireland, Dublin.

Ó Cofaigh, C., Dunlop, P., Benetti, S. 2010. Marine geophysical evidence for Late Pleistocene ice sheet extent and recession off northwest Ireland. *Quaternary Science Reviews* (in press).

O'Donovan, J. (editor and translator) 1856. *Annals of the Kingdom of Ireland by the Four Masters*, Dublin. (Reprinted 1966, AMS Press. New York).

PRONI, MPF 1/35, Public Records Office of Northern Ireland, *Generalle Description of Ulster*.

Royal Haskoning and McKenzie Wilson, 2008. Integrated Beach Management, Marine Leisure and Tourism Initiative for Rathmullan, Co. Donegal. Feasibility Study.

Slesser, G. and Turrell, W.R. 2005. Annual cycles of physical chemicals and biological parameters in Scottish waters (2005 update). *FRS Internal Report*, 19:05.

Swan H.P. 1949. *Twist Foyle and Swilly*. Hodges Figgis, Dublin.

Went, A.E.J. 1966. Historical notes on the fisheries of Lough Swilly and its tributaries. *Journal of the Royal Society of Antiquaries of Ireland*, 96, 121–31.

Went, A.E.J. 1971. A fish pond in Lough Swilly in 1739. *Journal of the Royal Society of Antiquaries*, 101, 166–7.

Woodman, P. 1978. *The Mesolithic in Ireland*, British Archaeological Reports, 58. Oxford.

Index

Page references in italics refer to illustrations